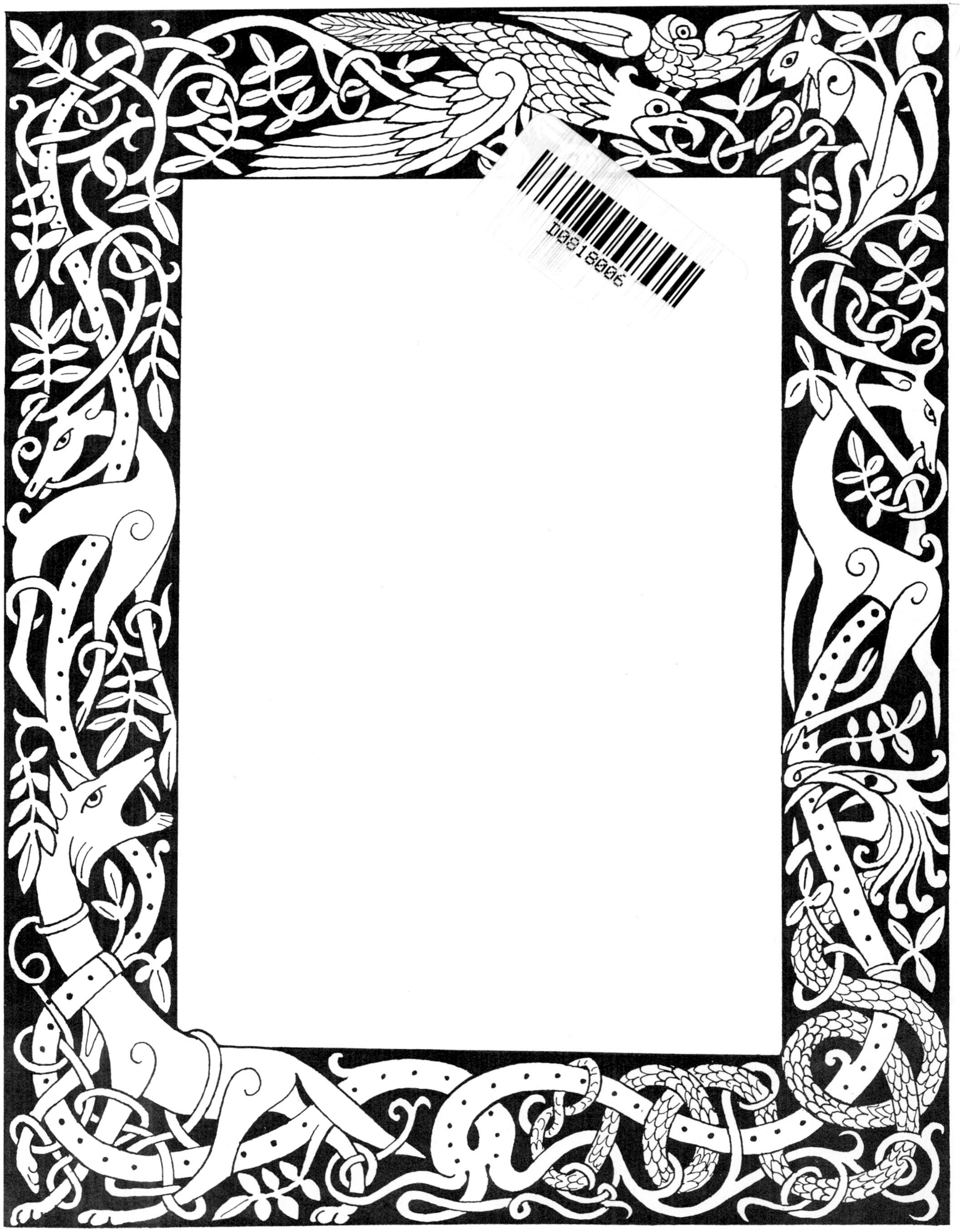

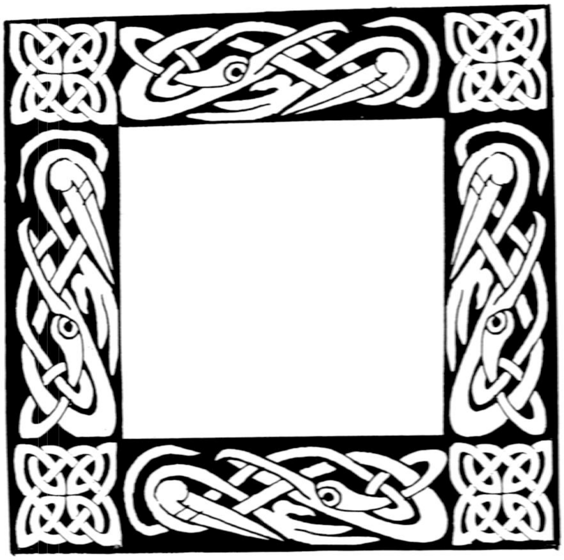

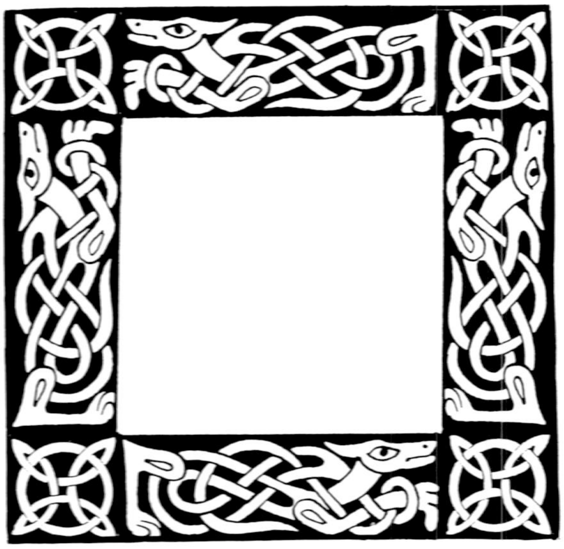

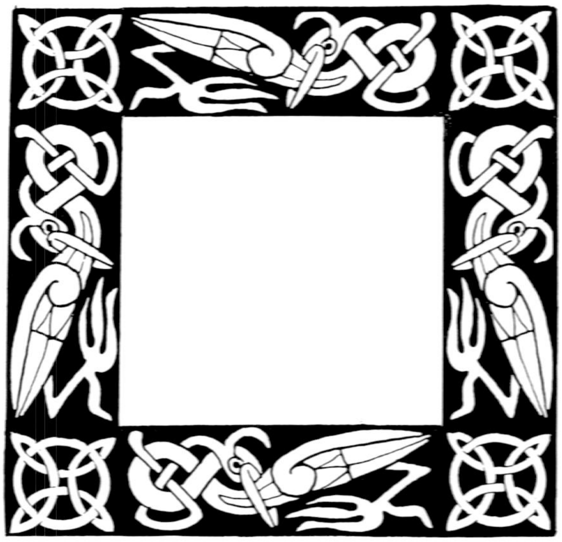

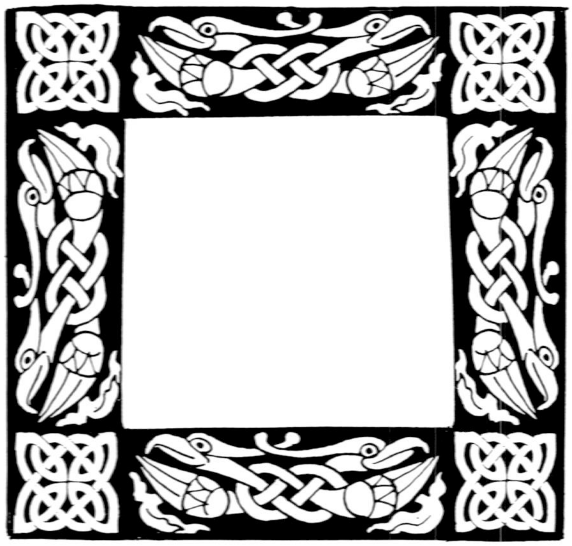

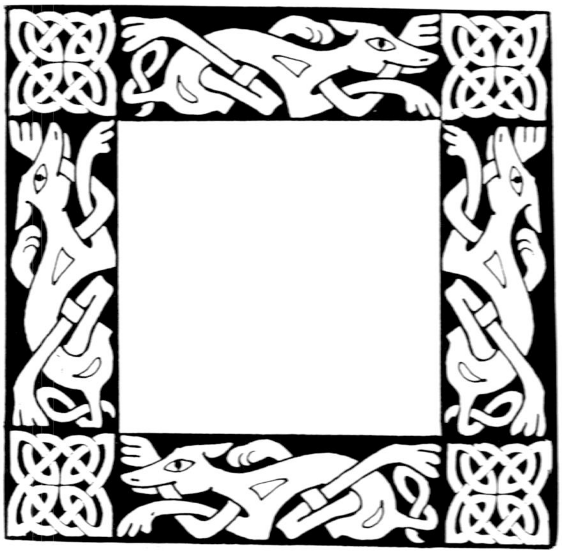

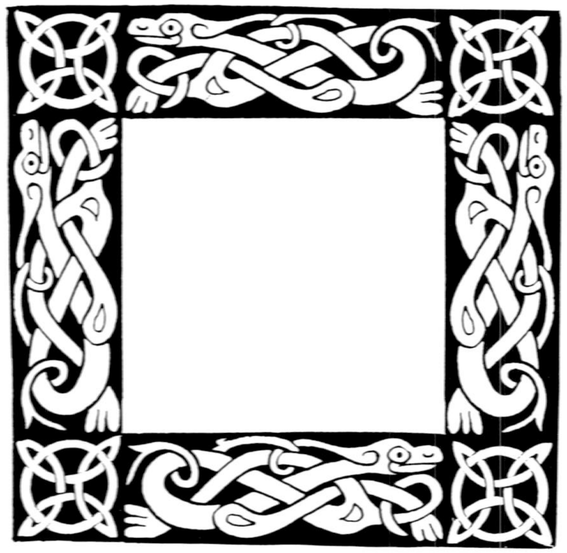

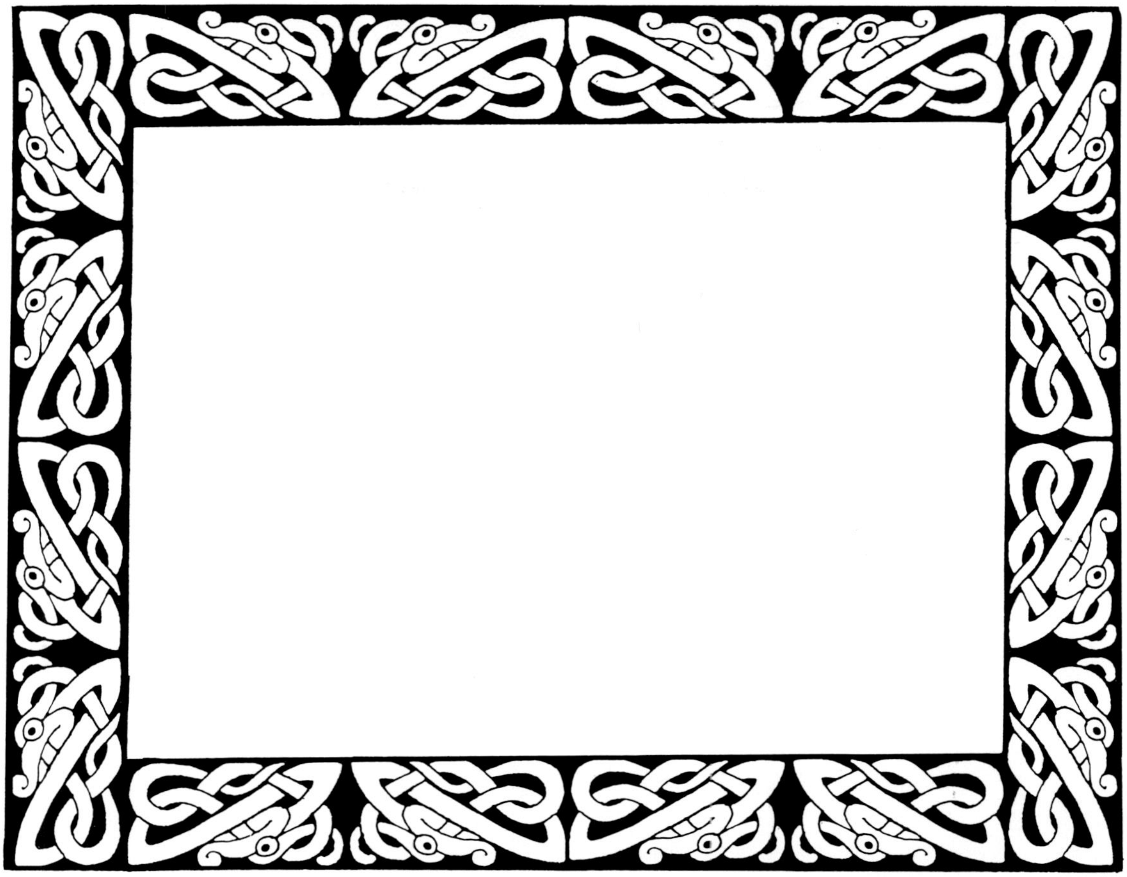

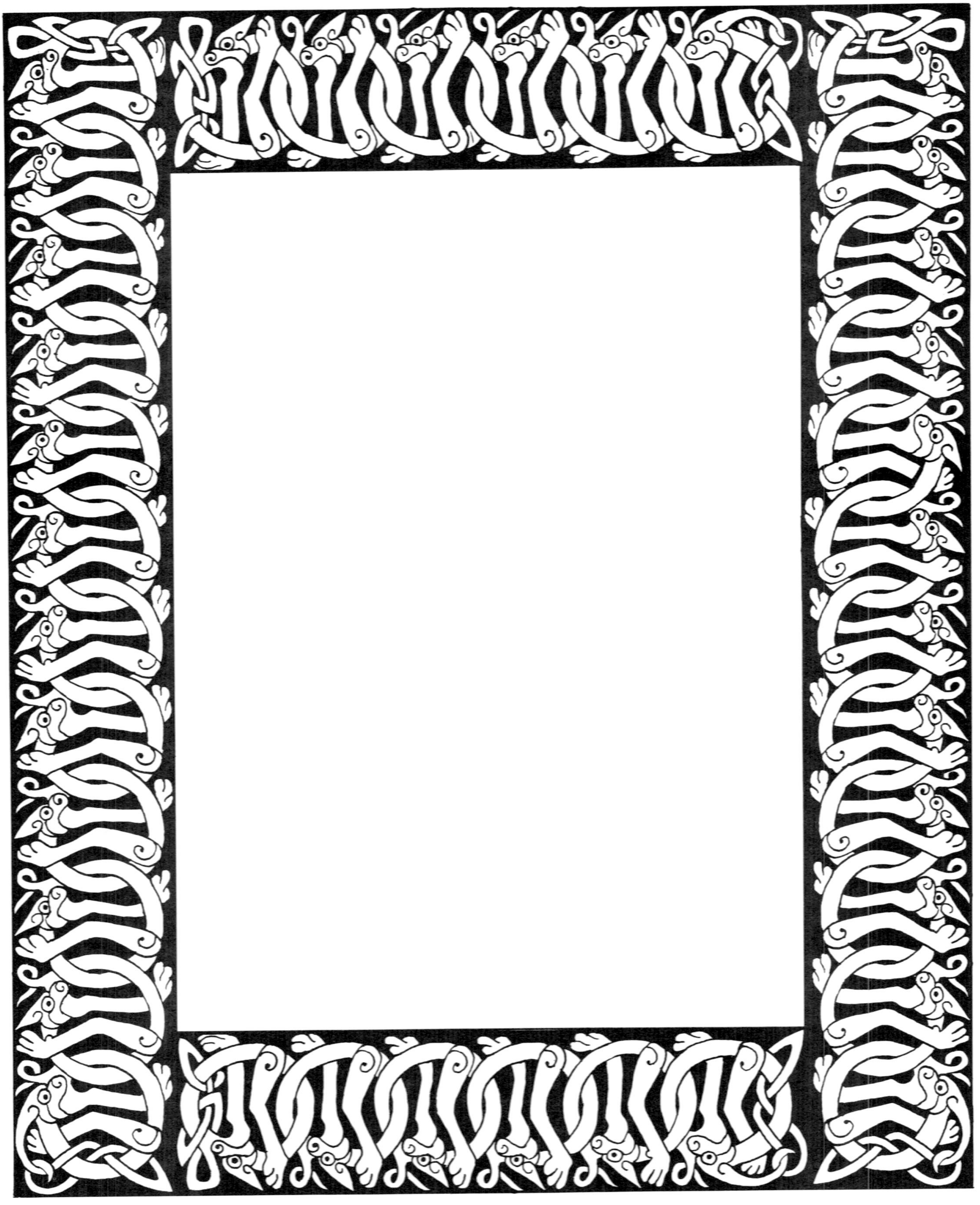

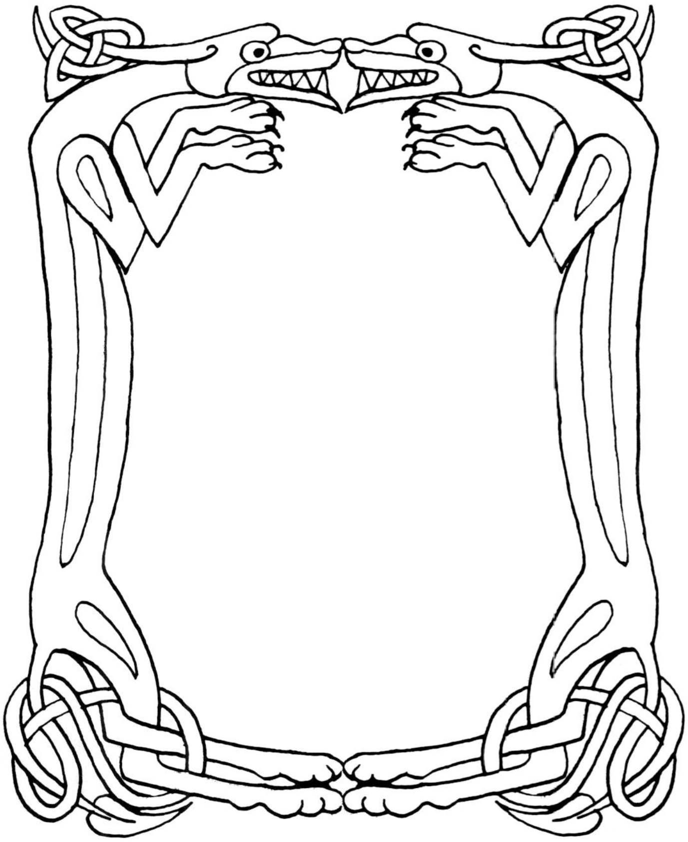
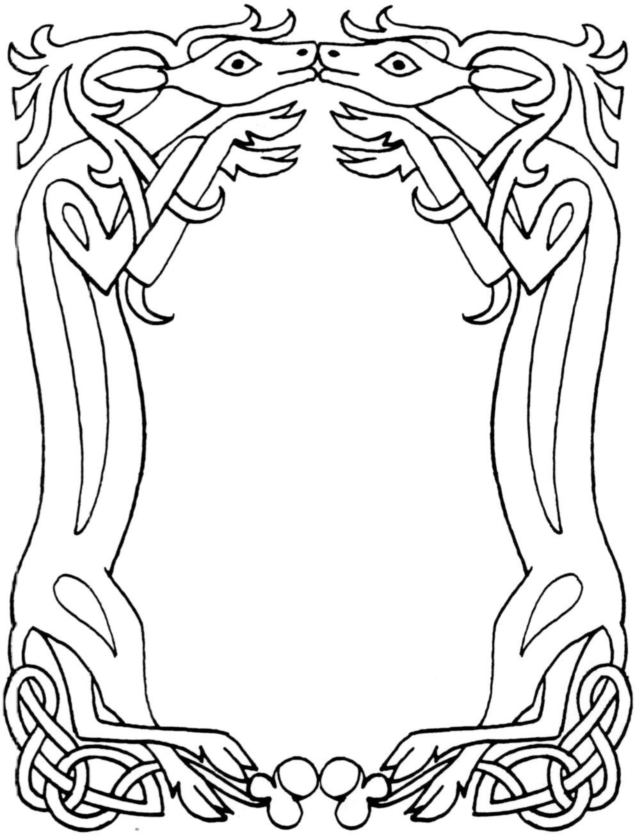
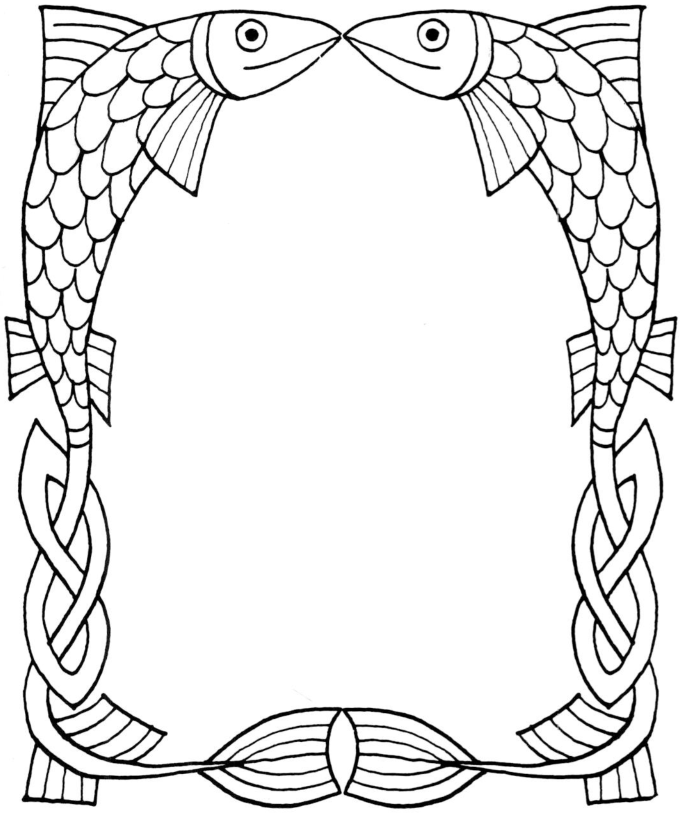
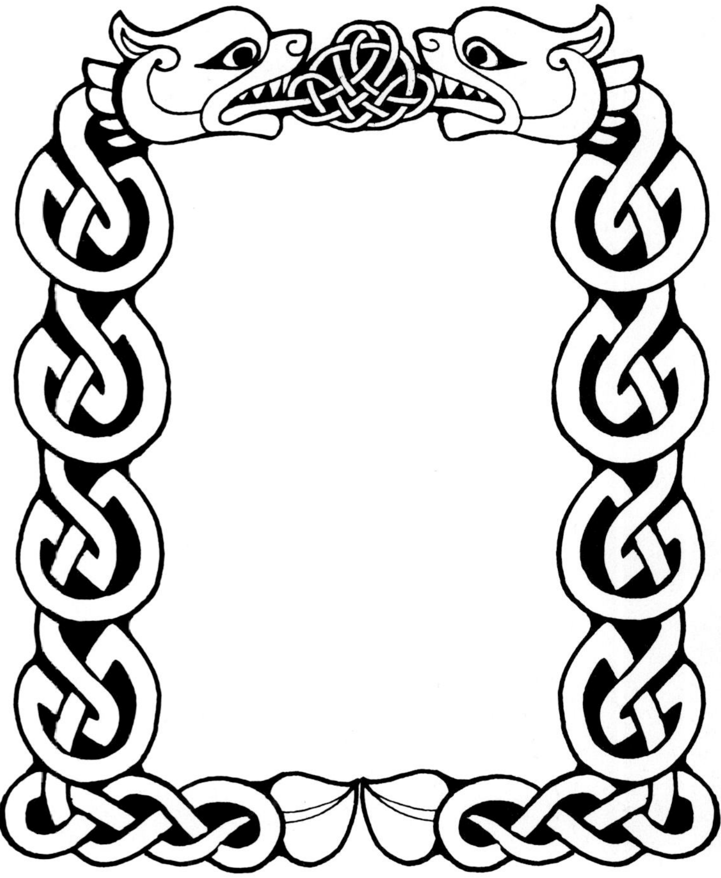

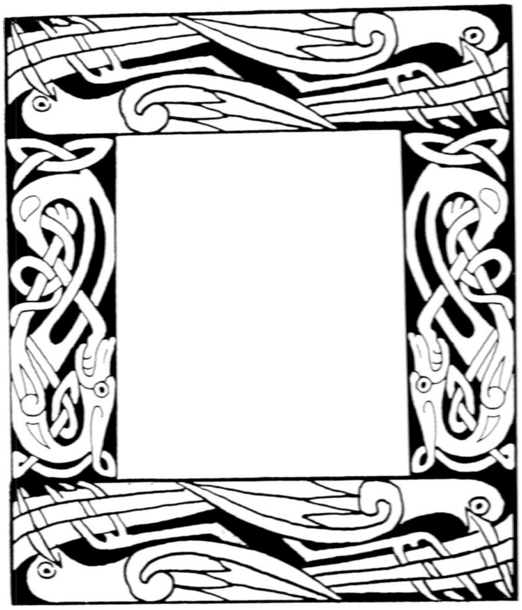
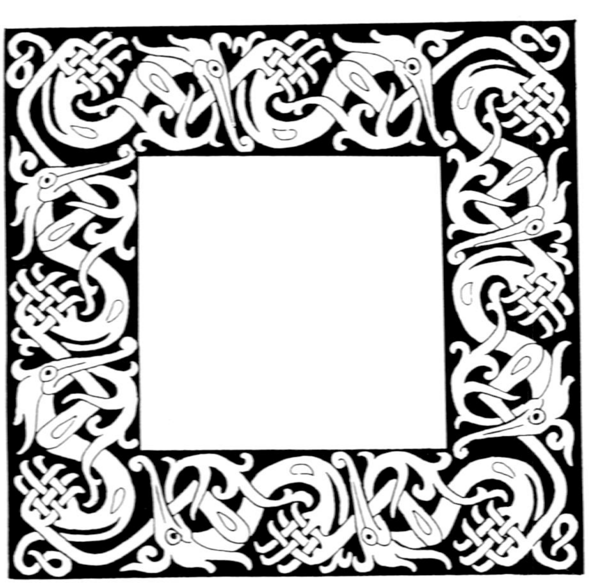
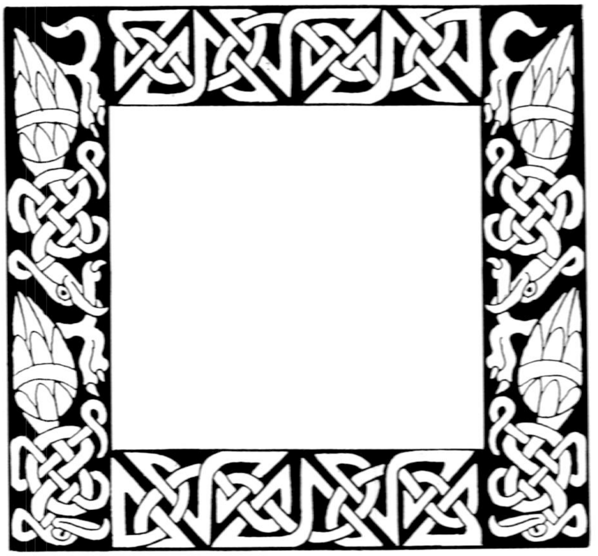
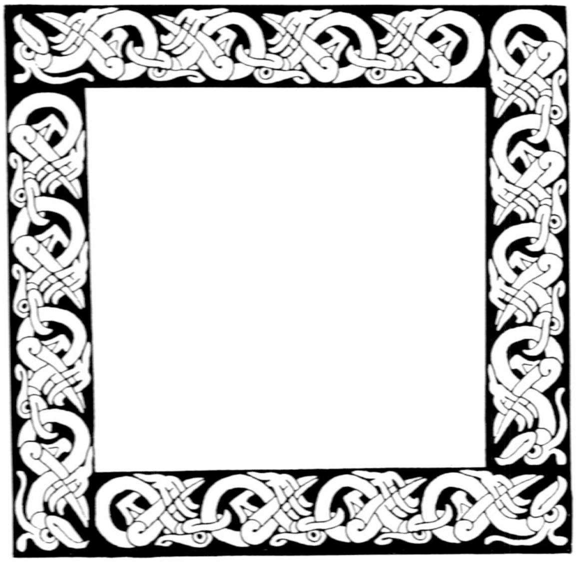
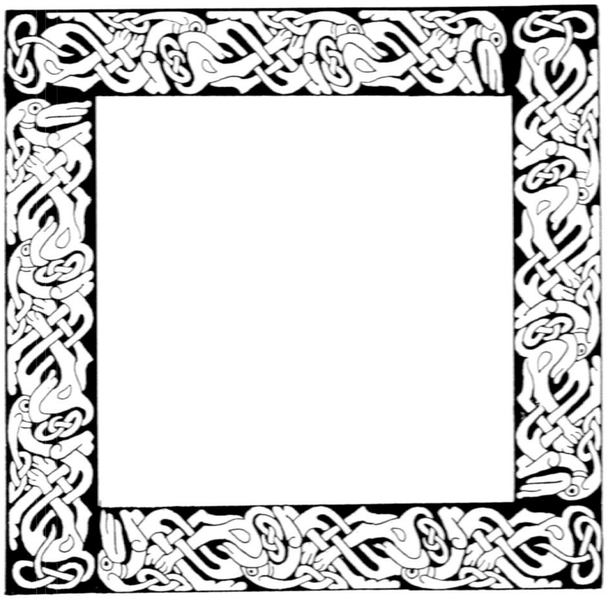
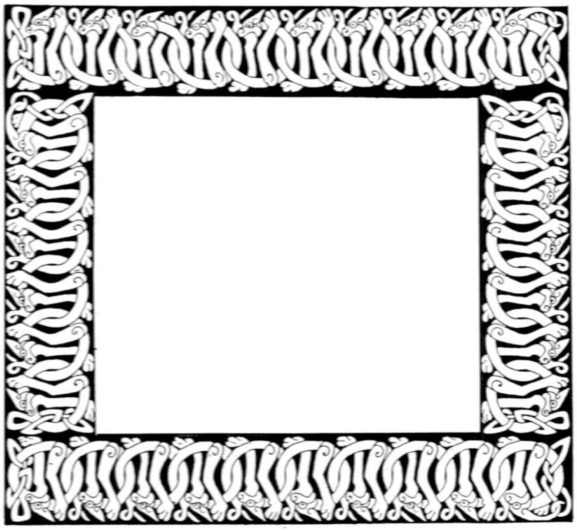

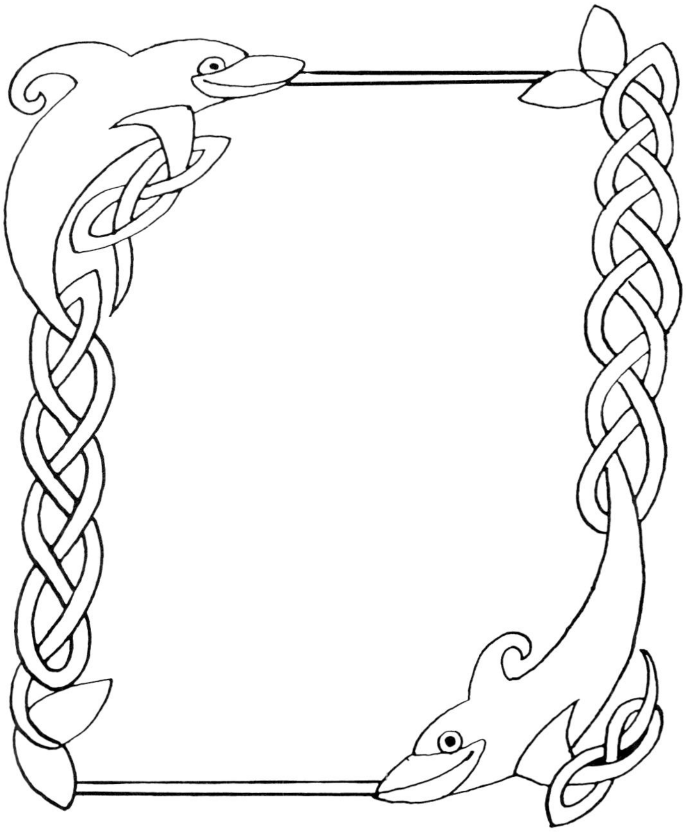
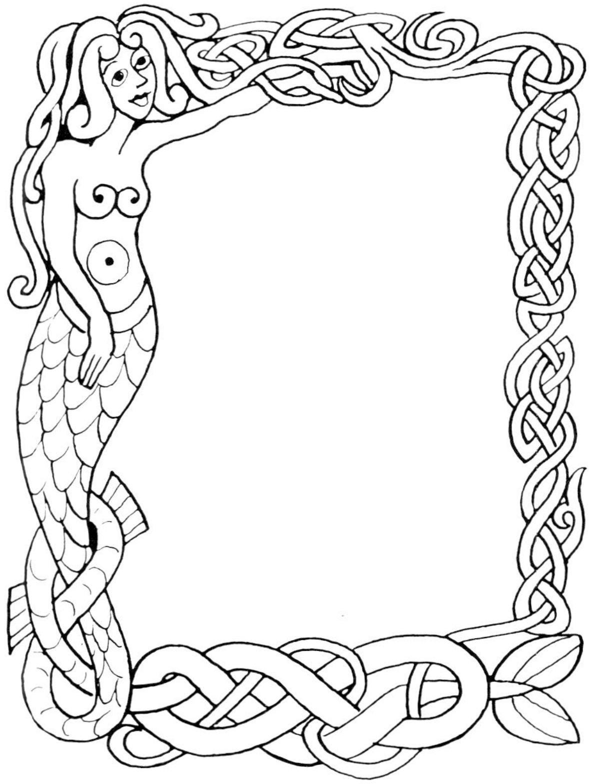
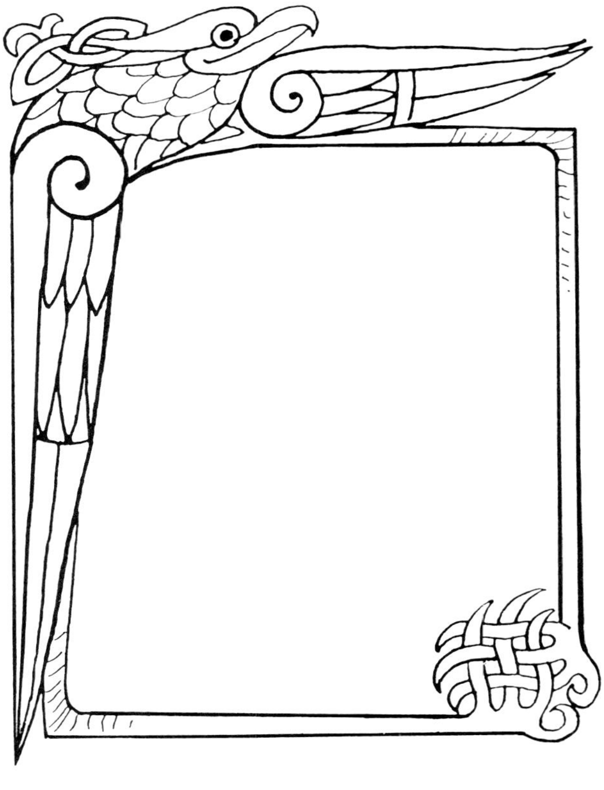
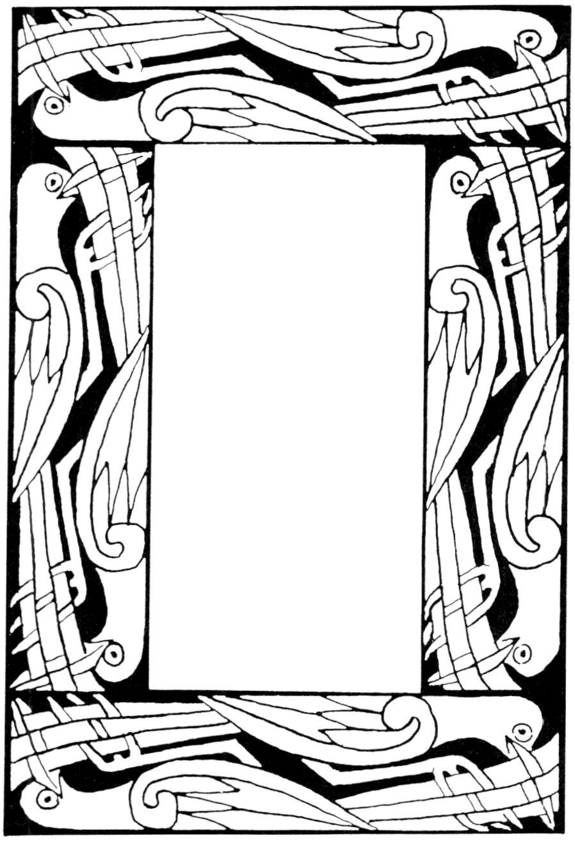

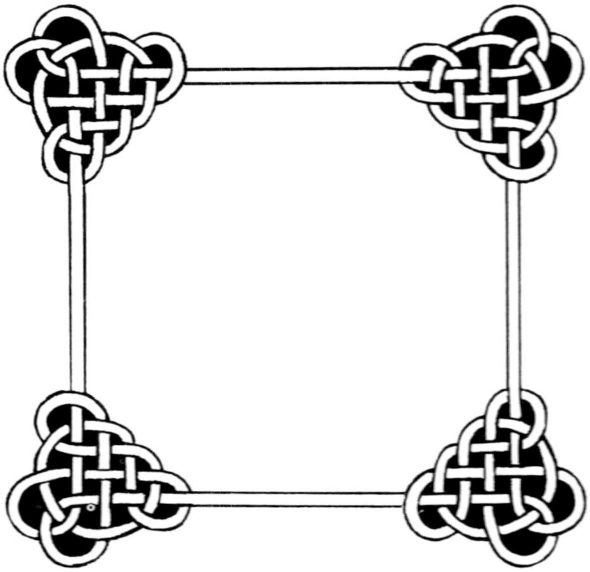
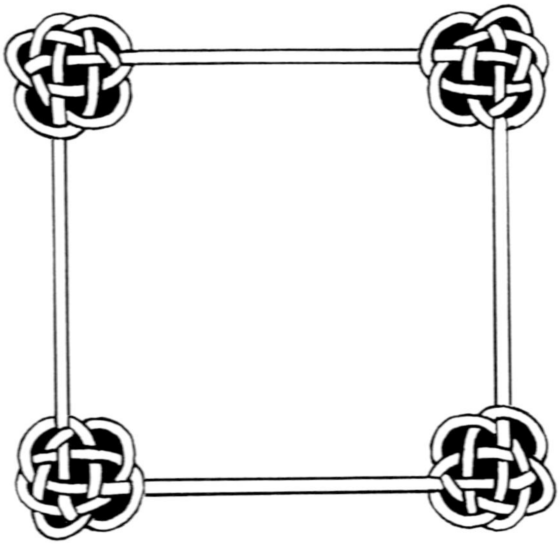
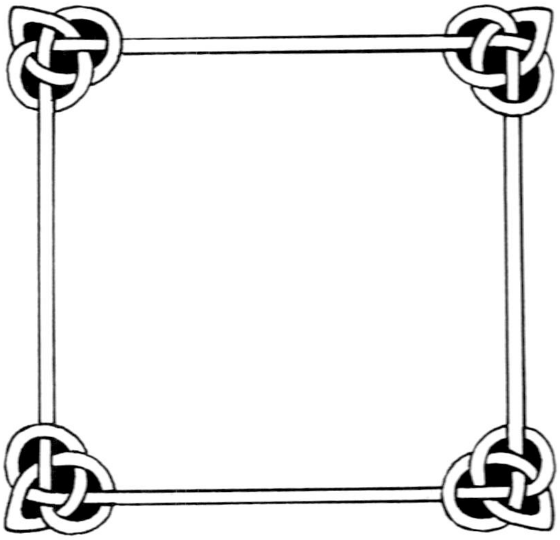
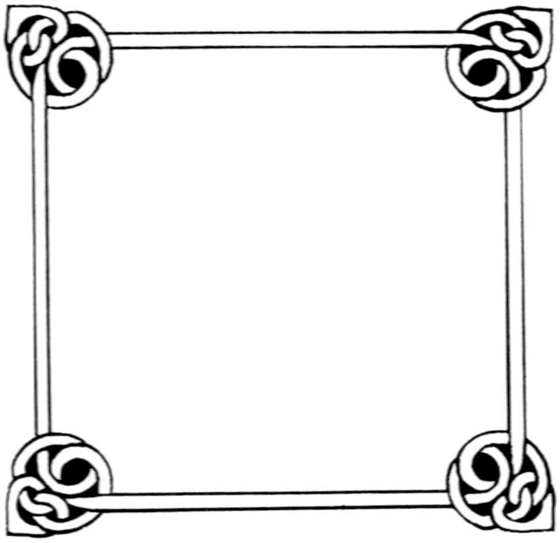
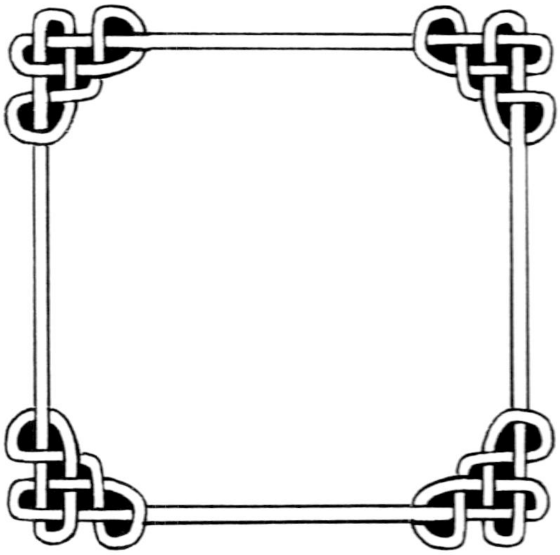
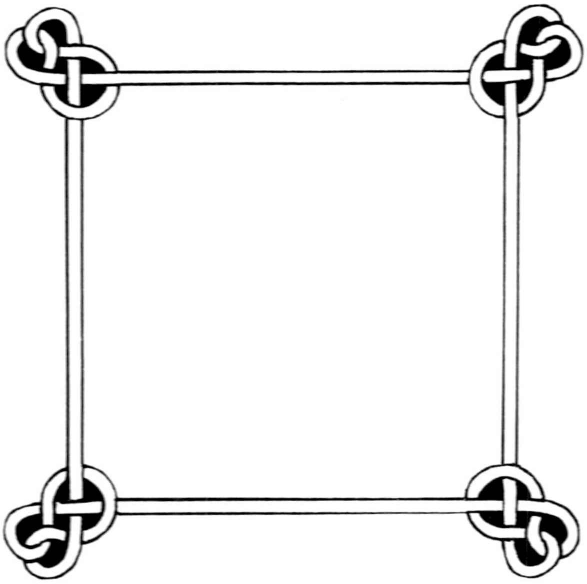

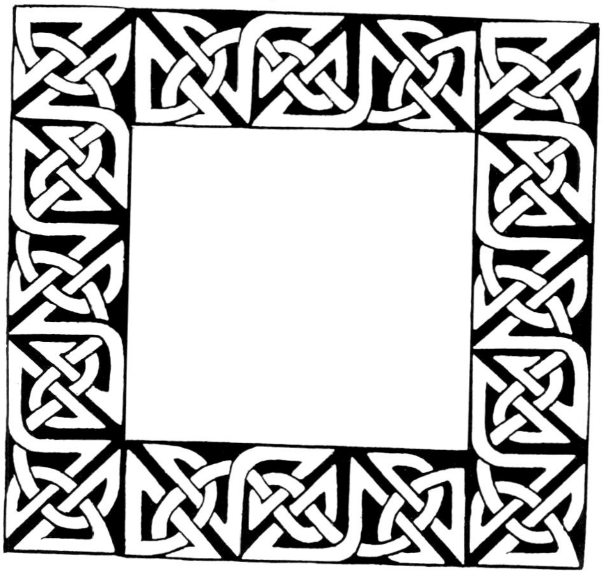

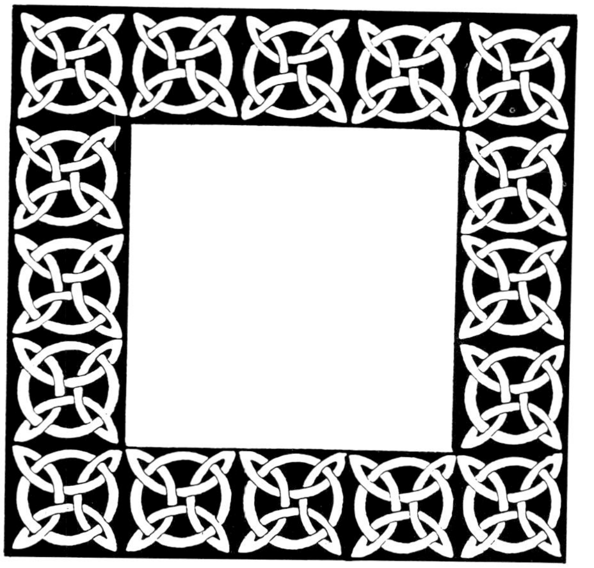

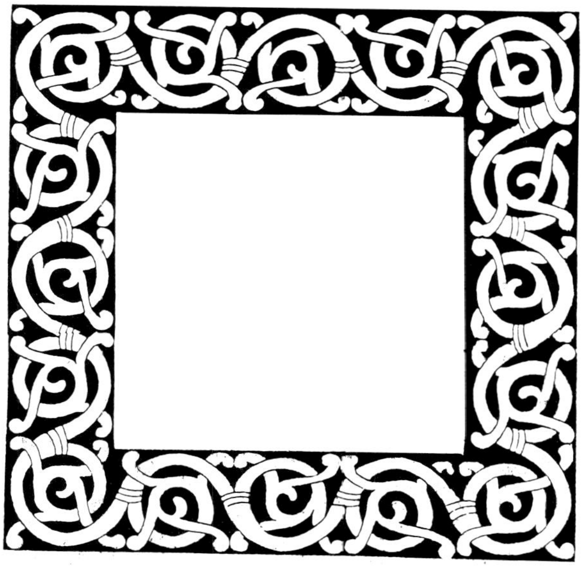

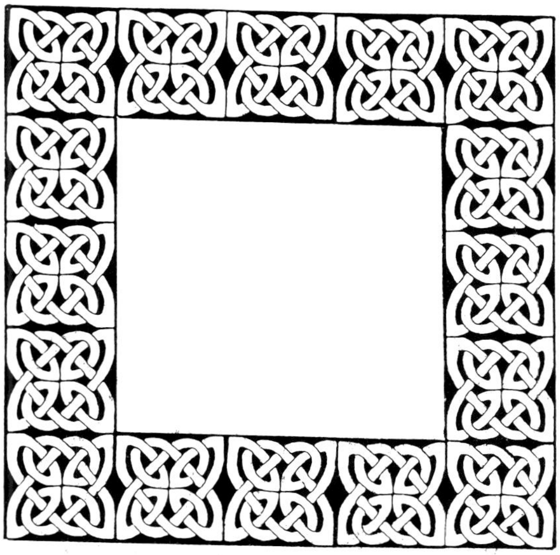

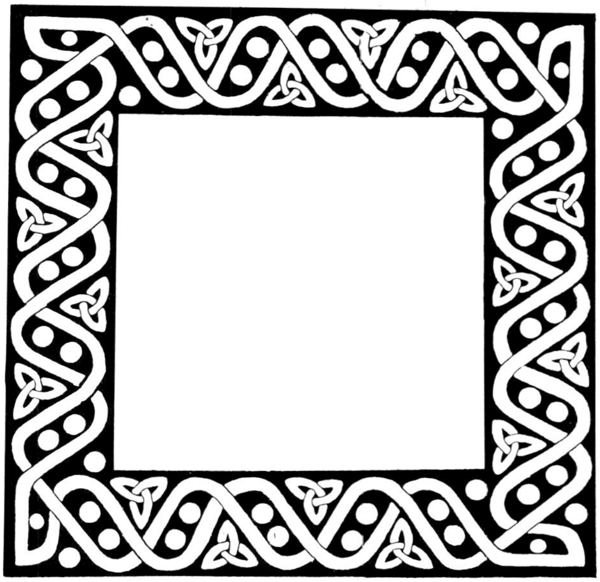

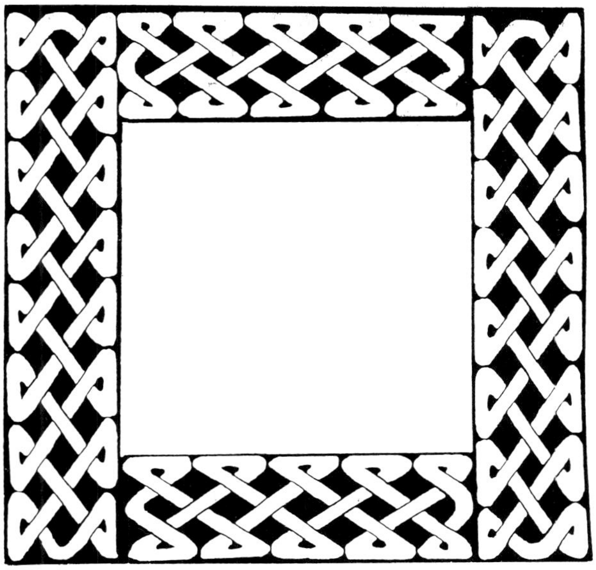

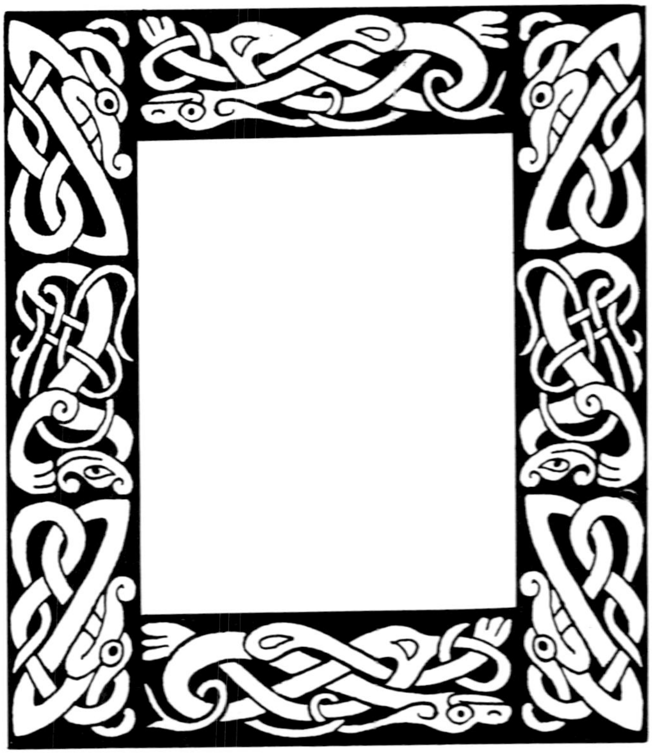
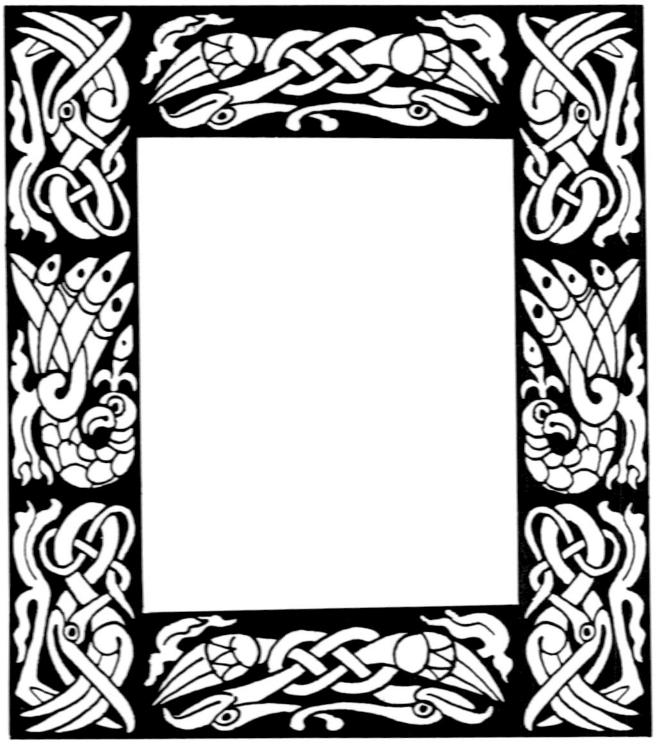
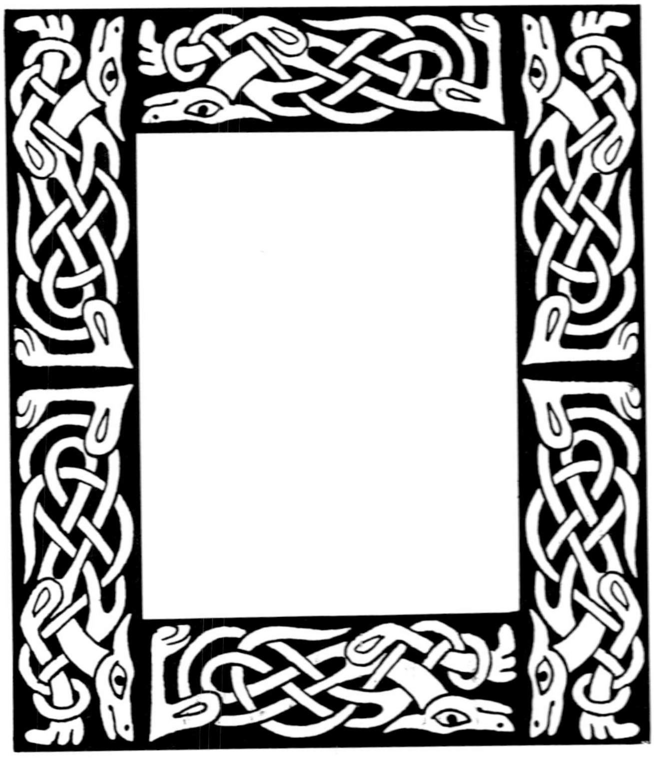
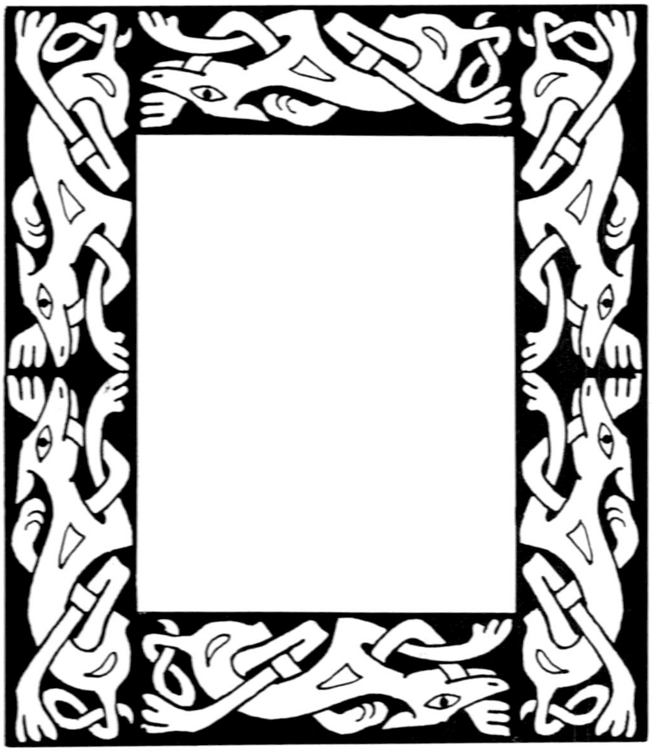

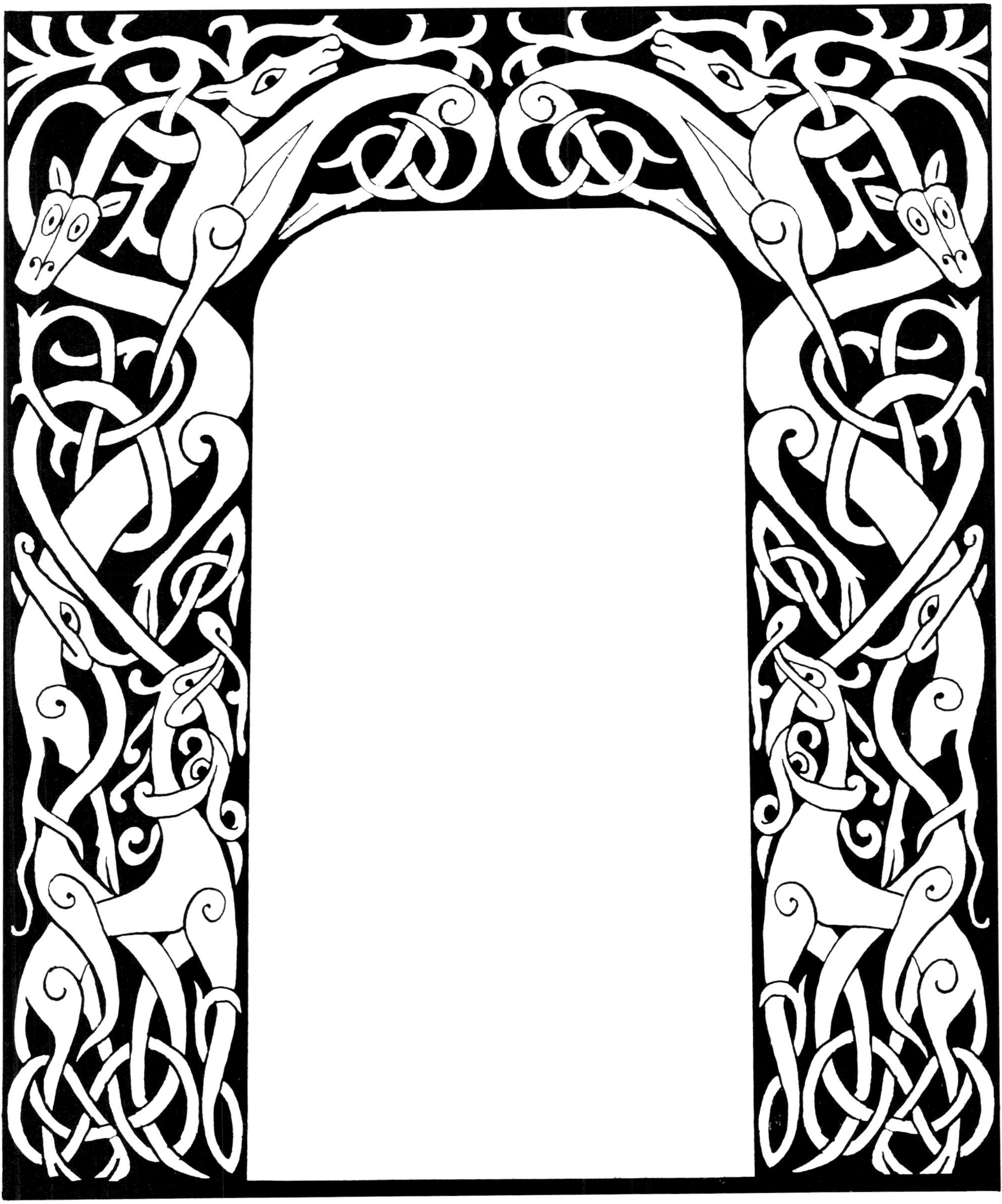

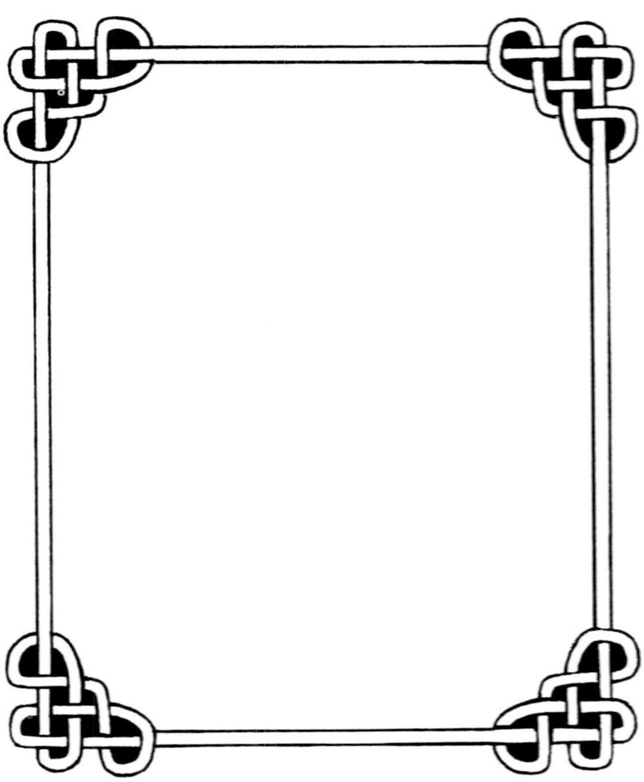

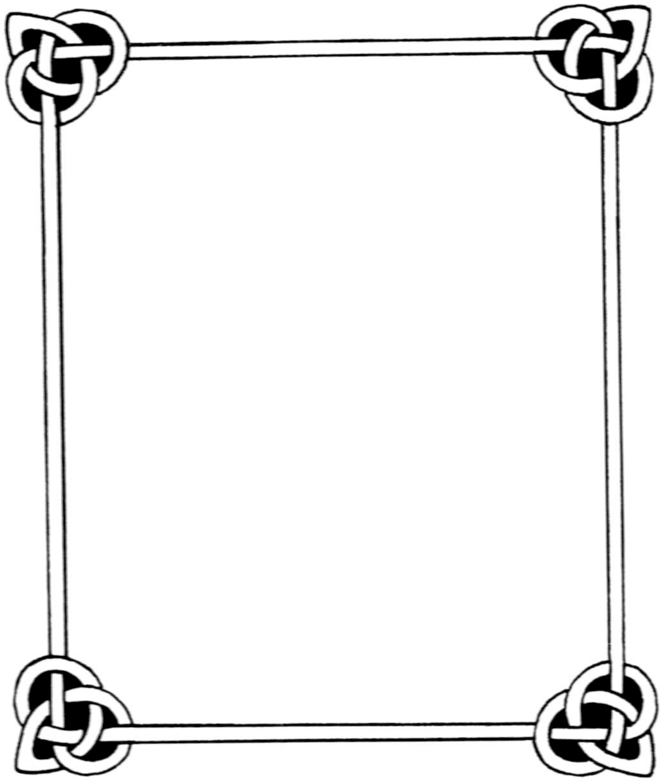

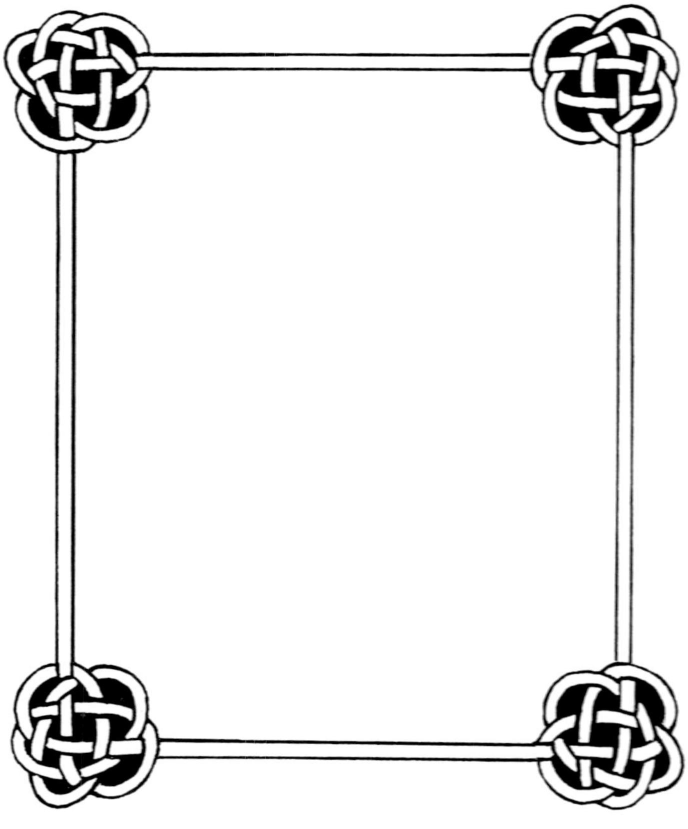

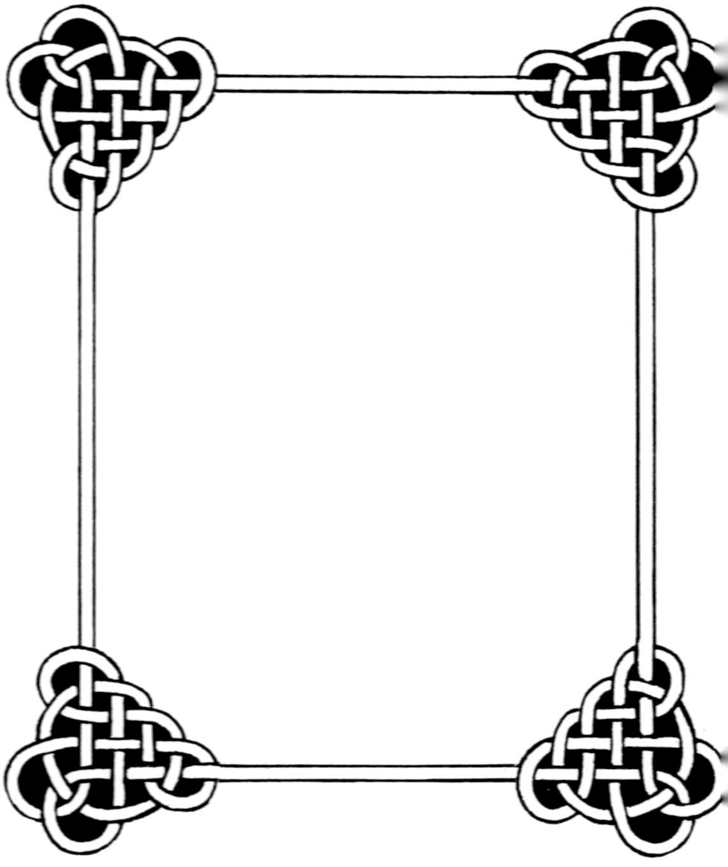

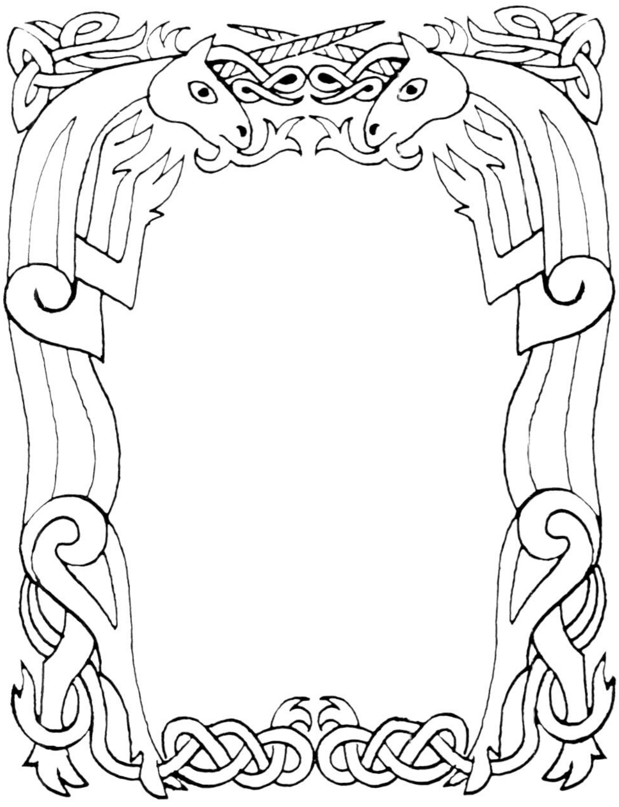
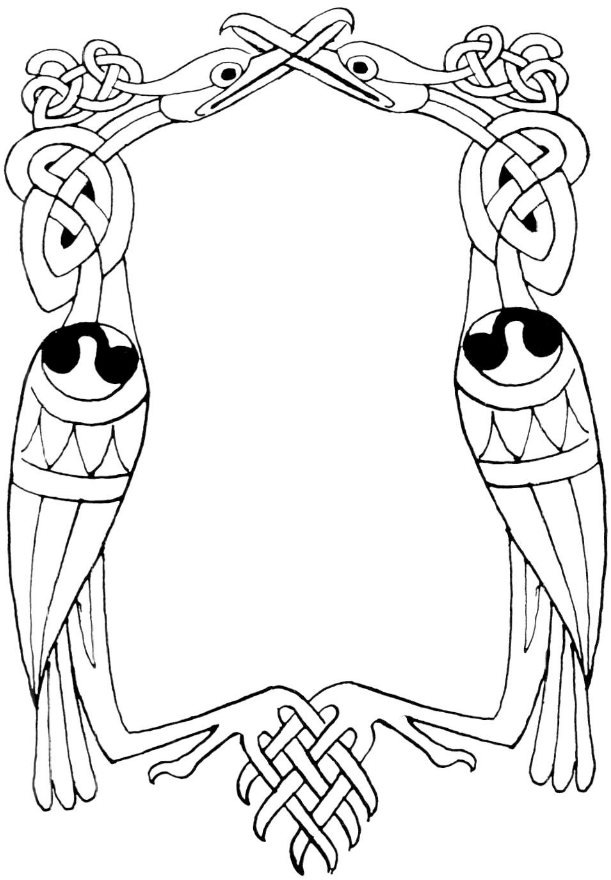
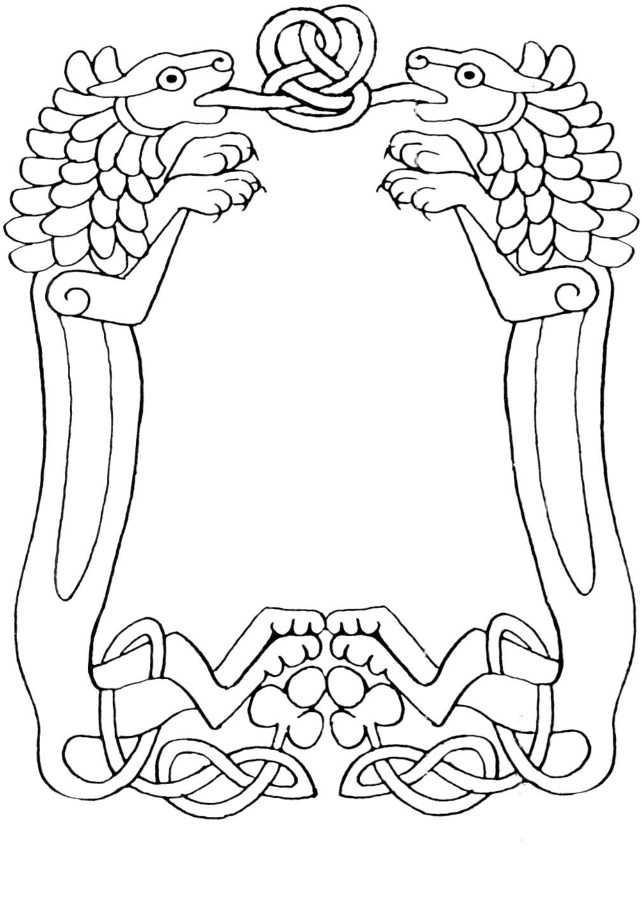
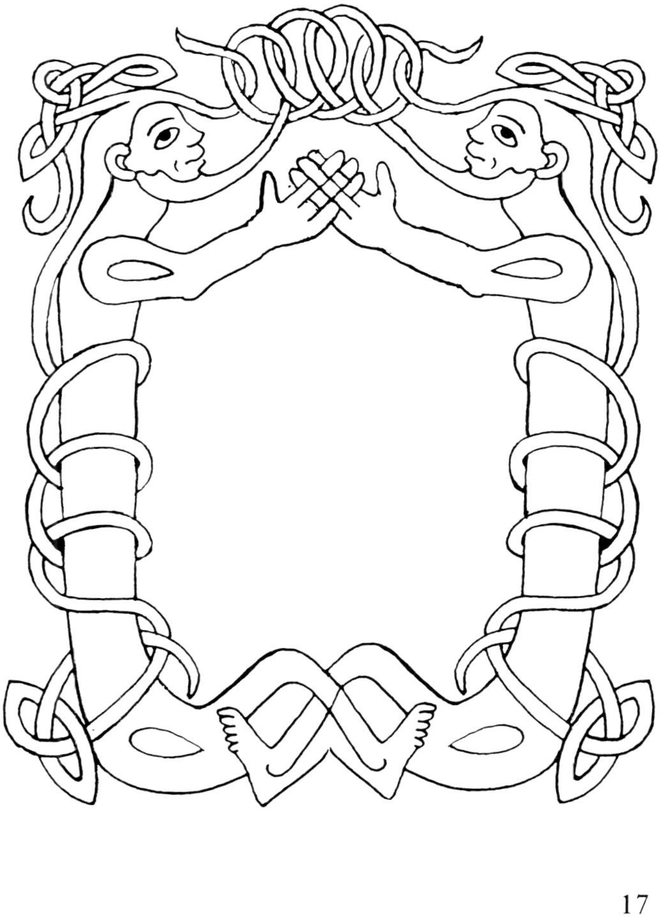

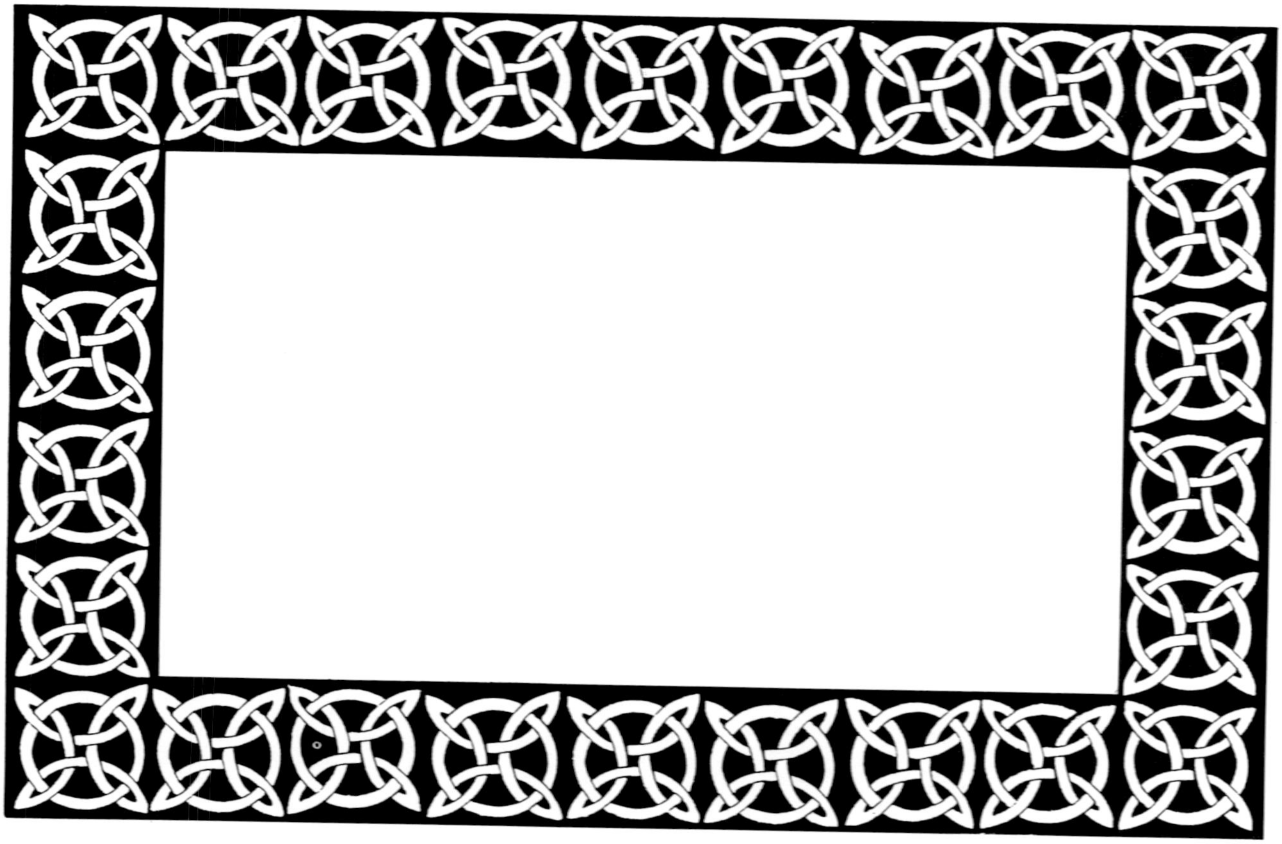

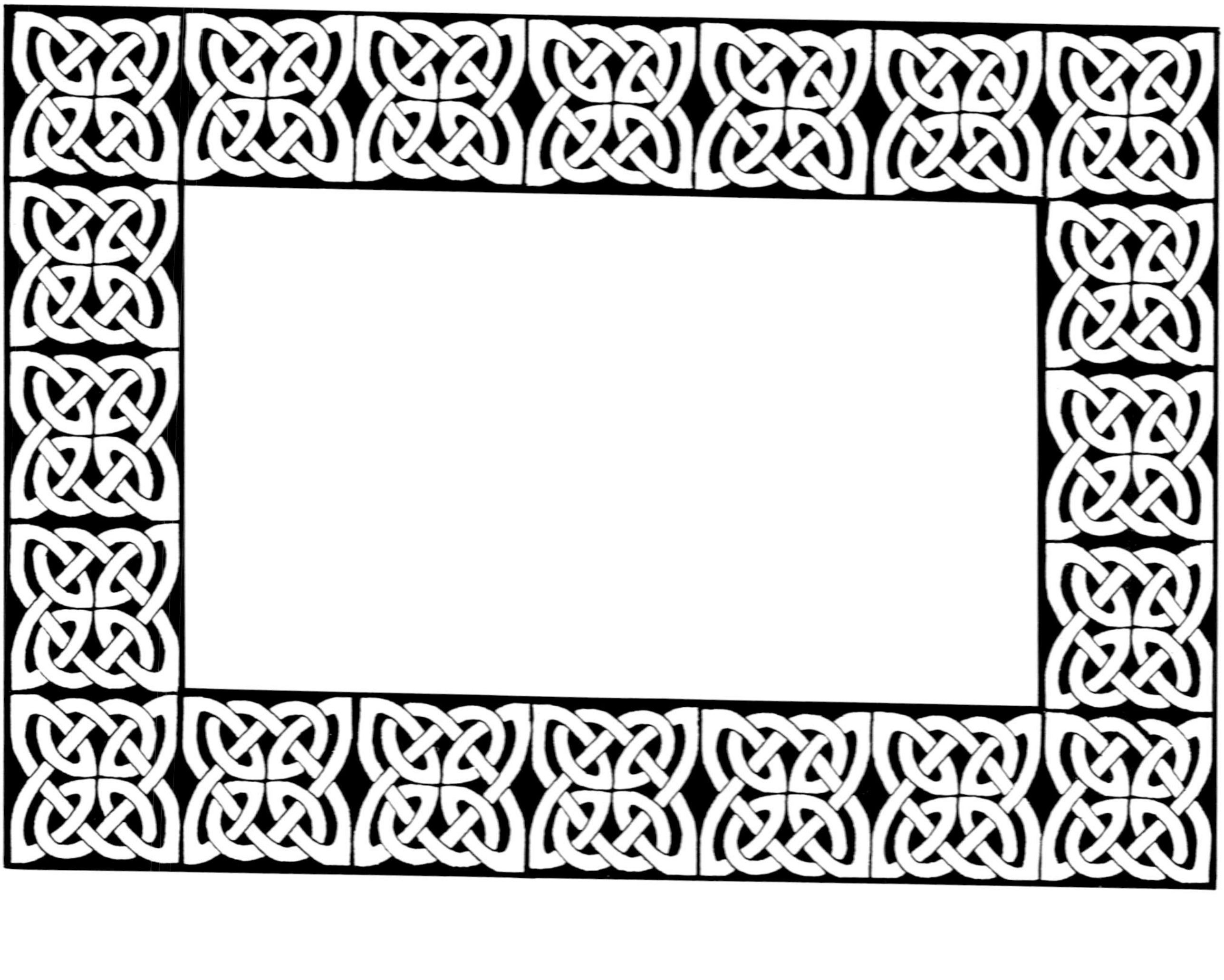

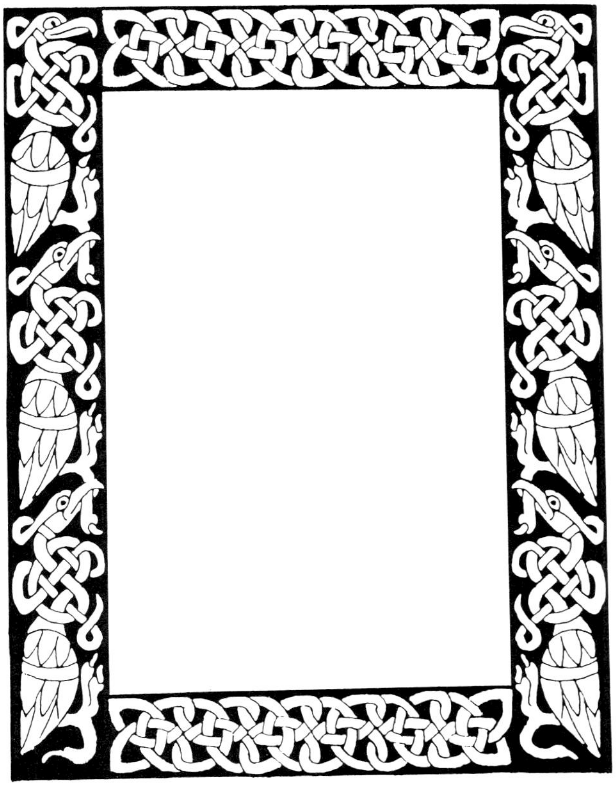

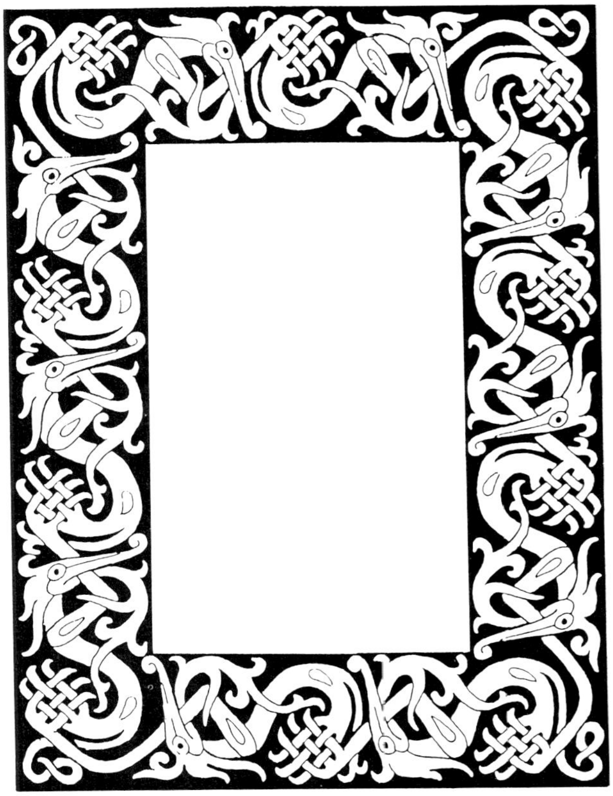

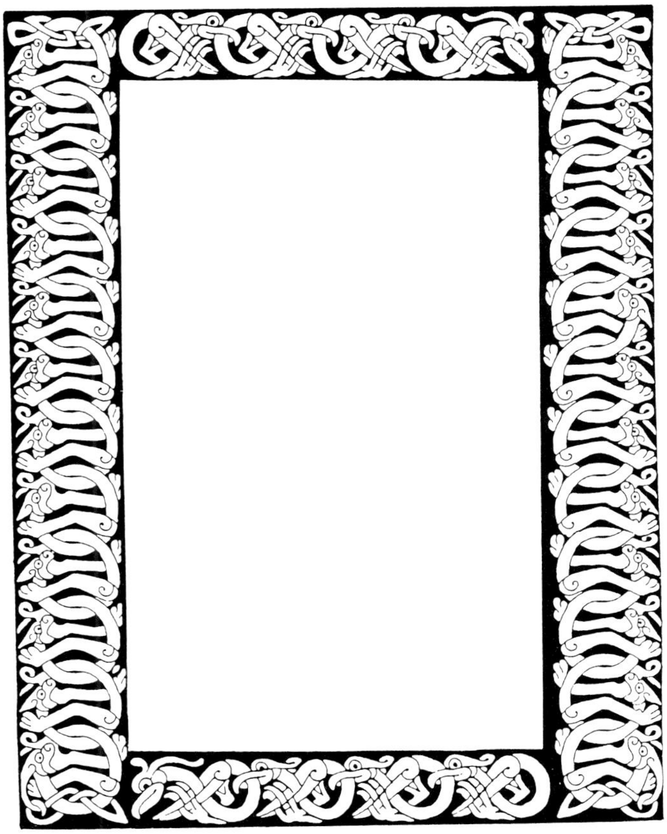

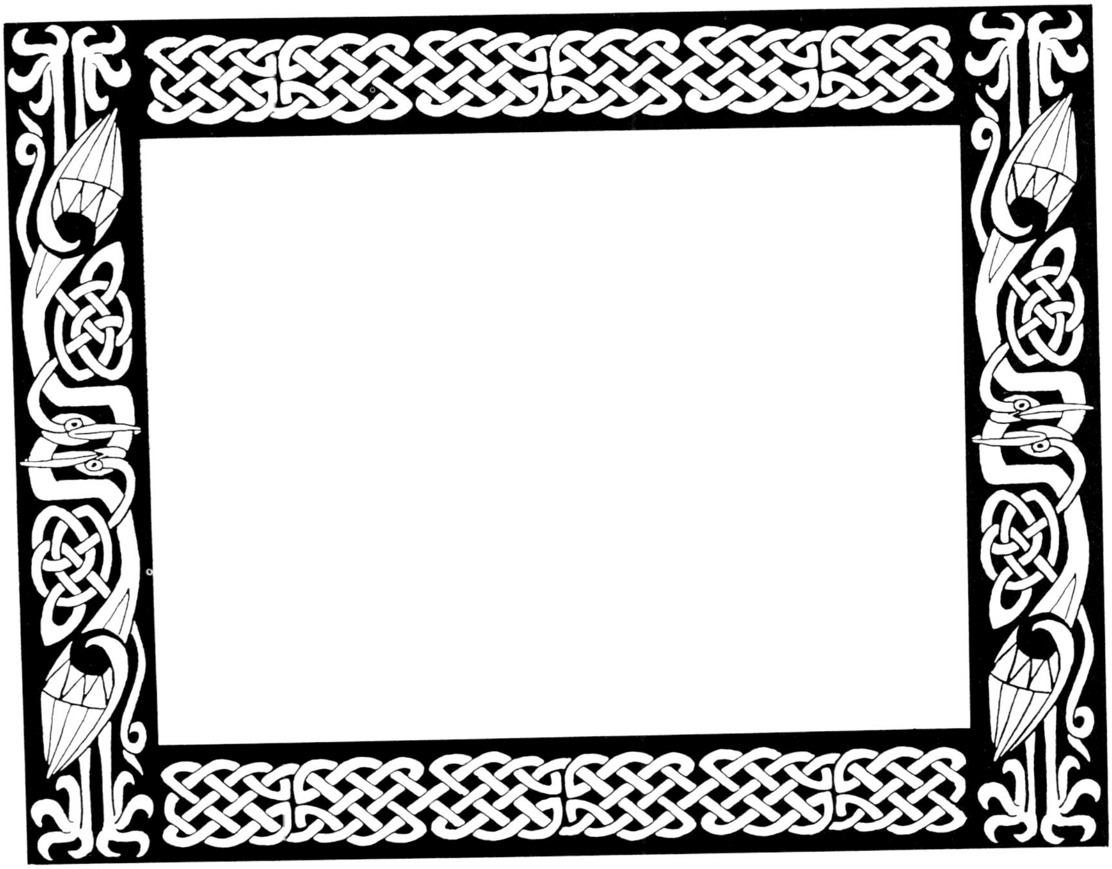

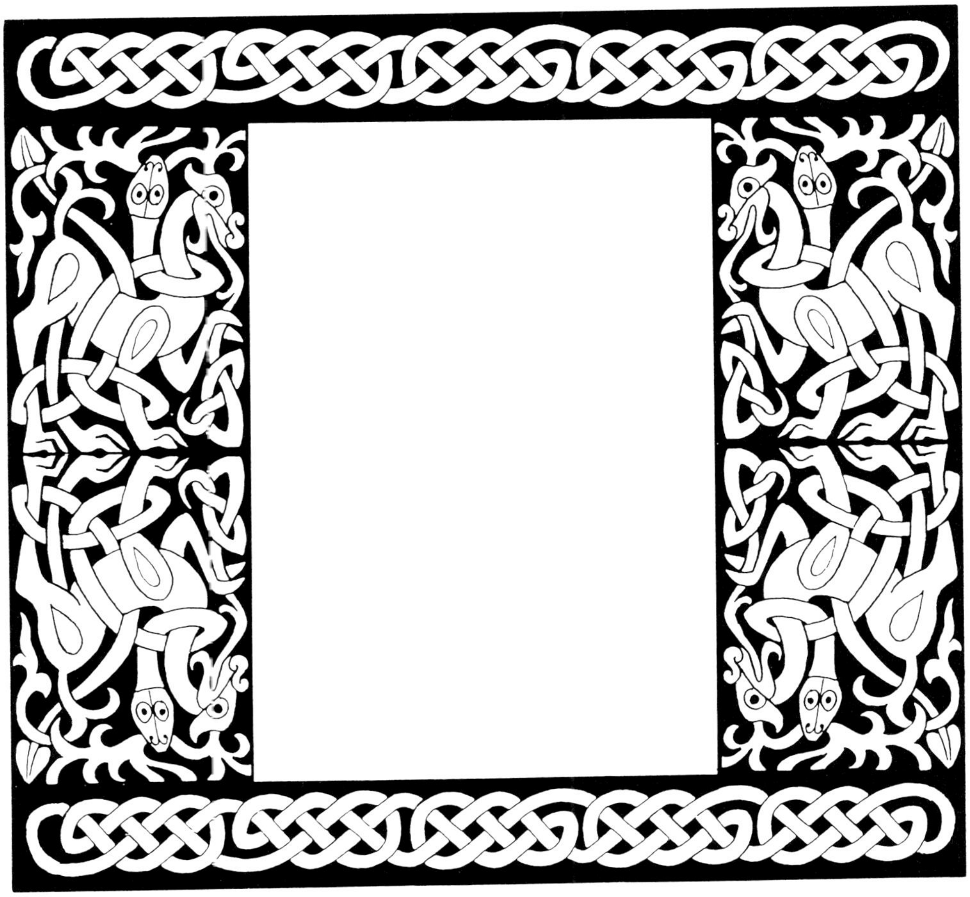

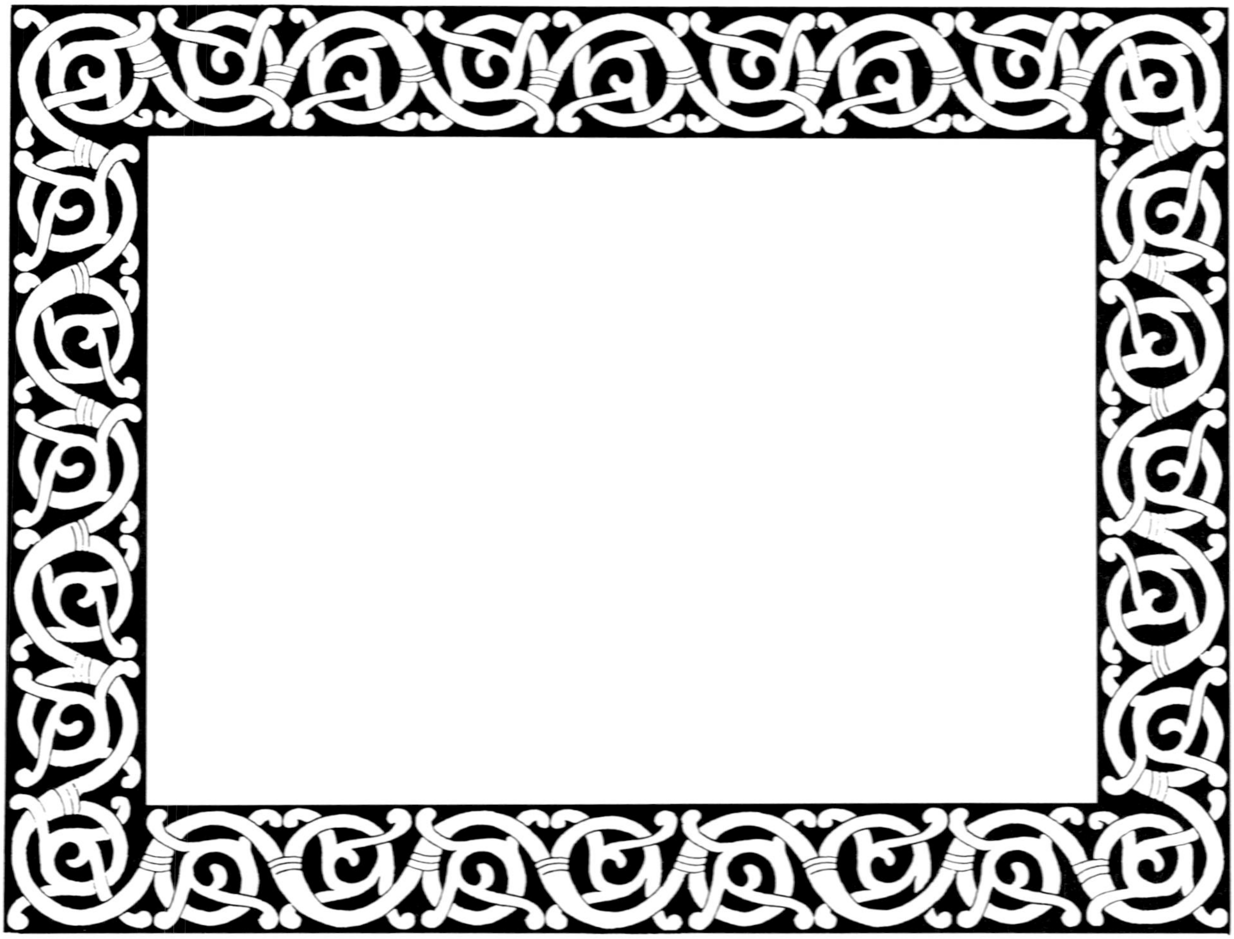

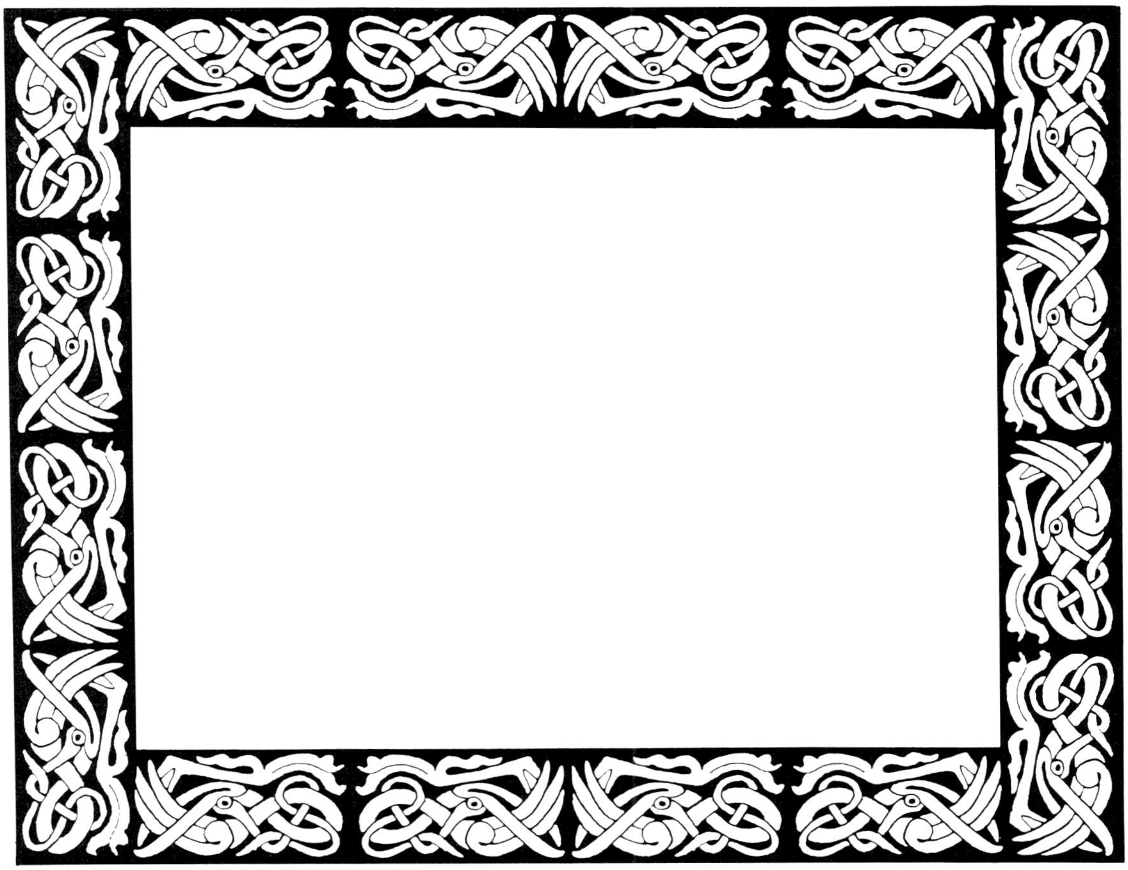

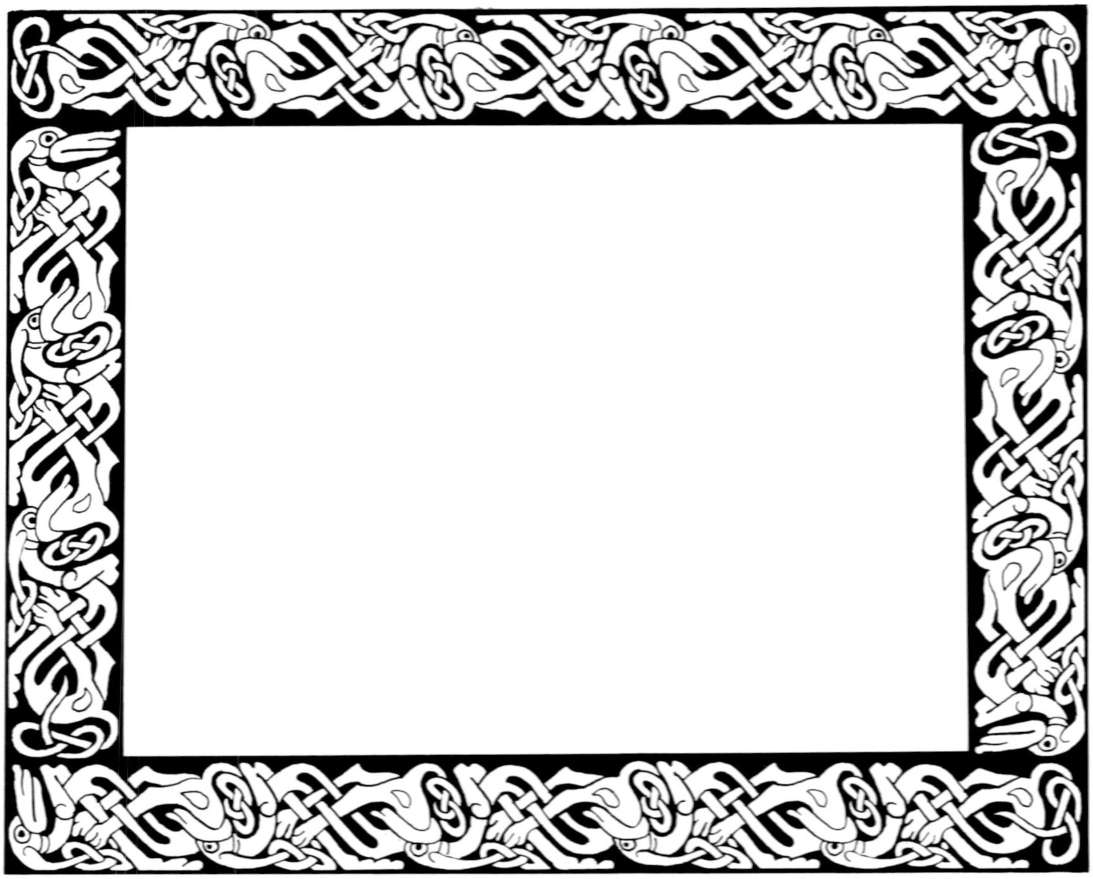

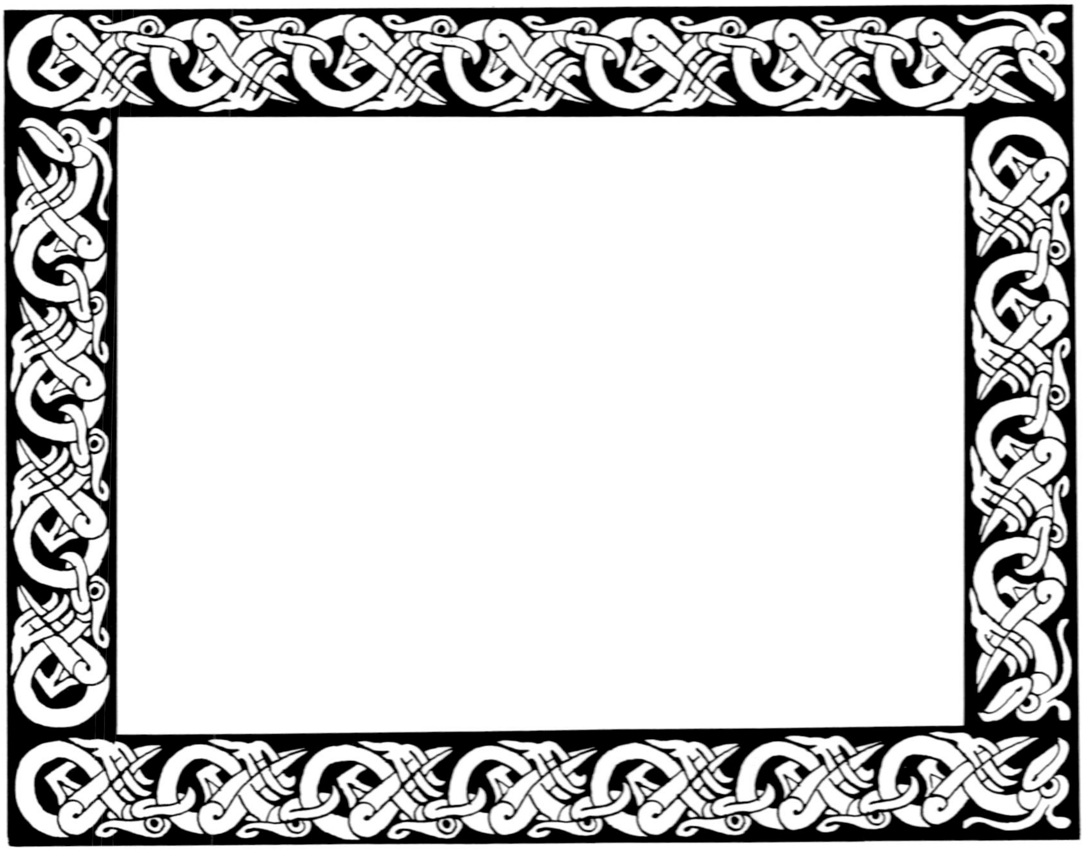

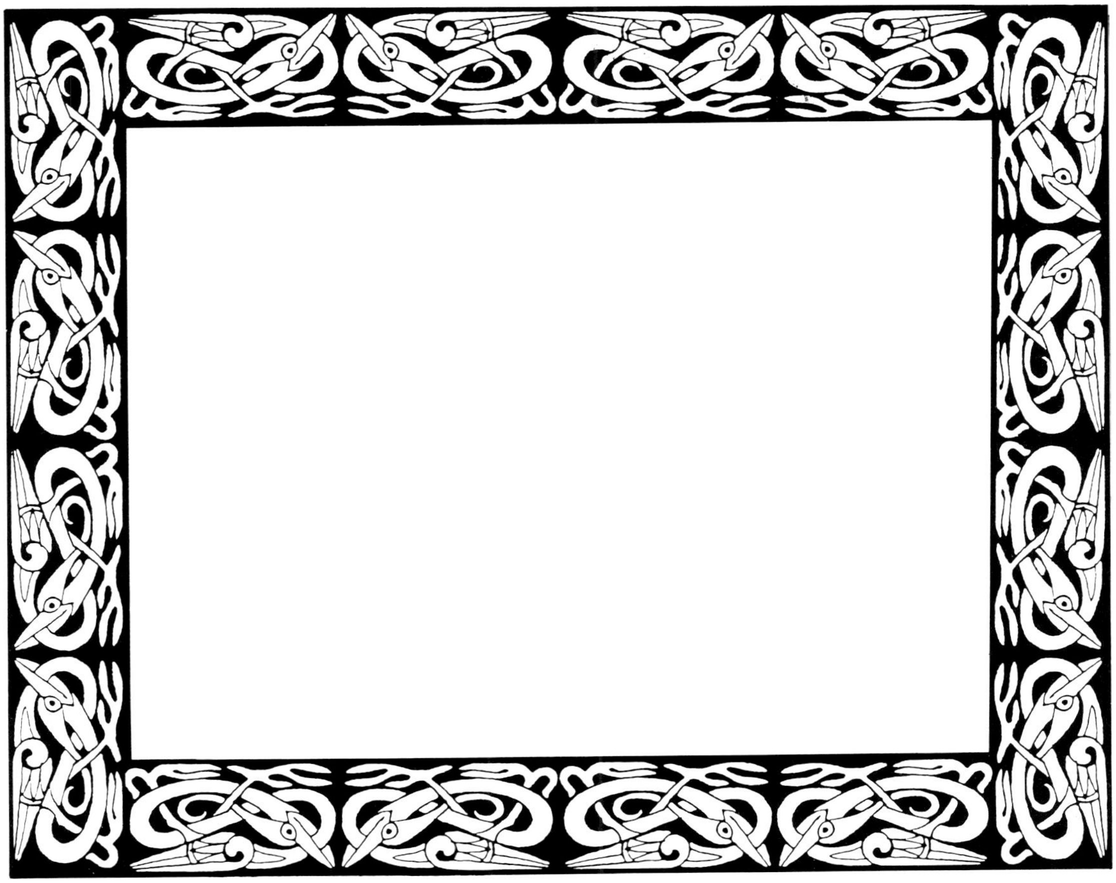

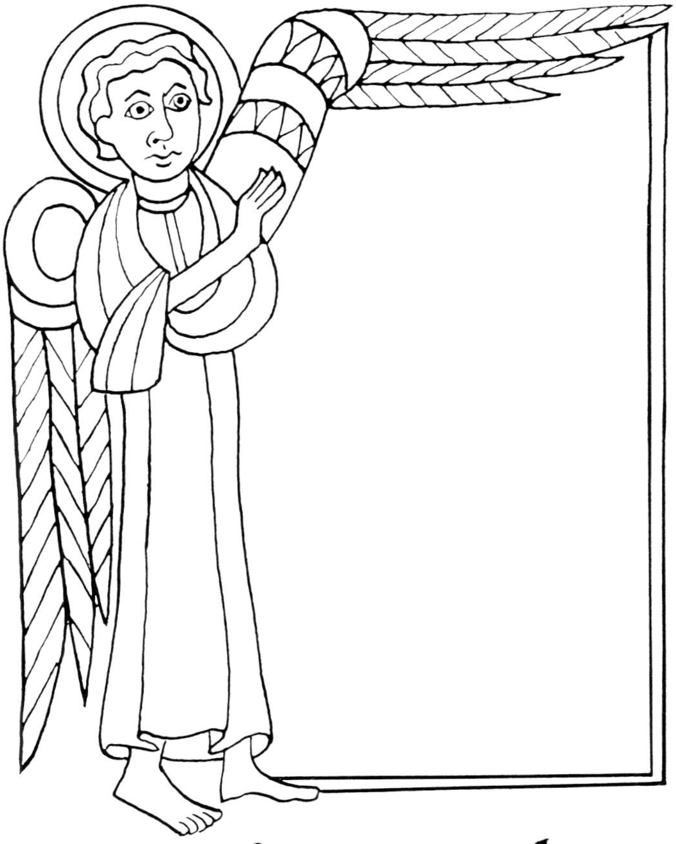

symbol for St. Matthew

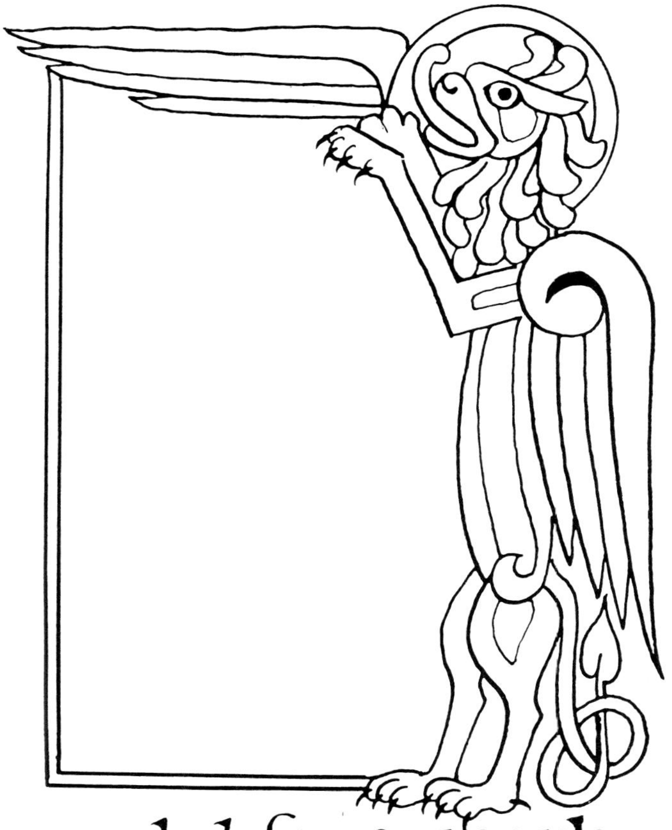

symbol for St. Mark

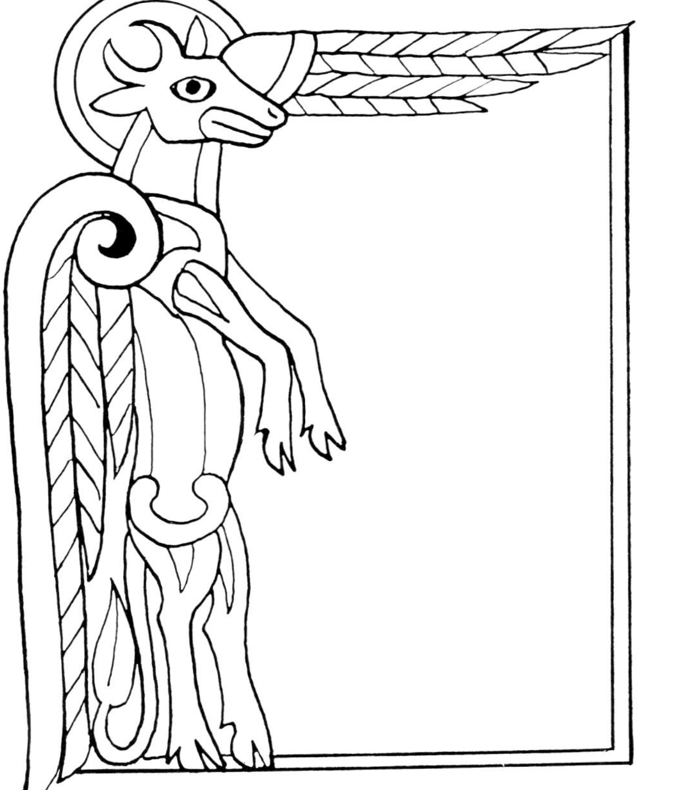

symbol for St. Luke

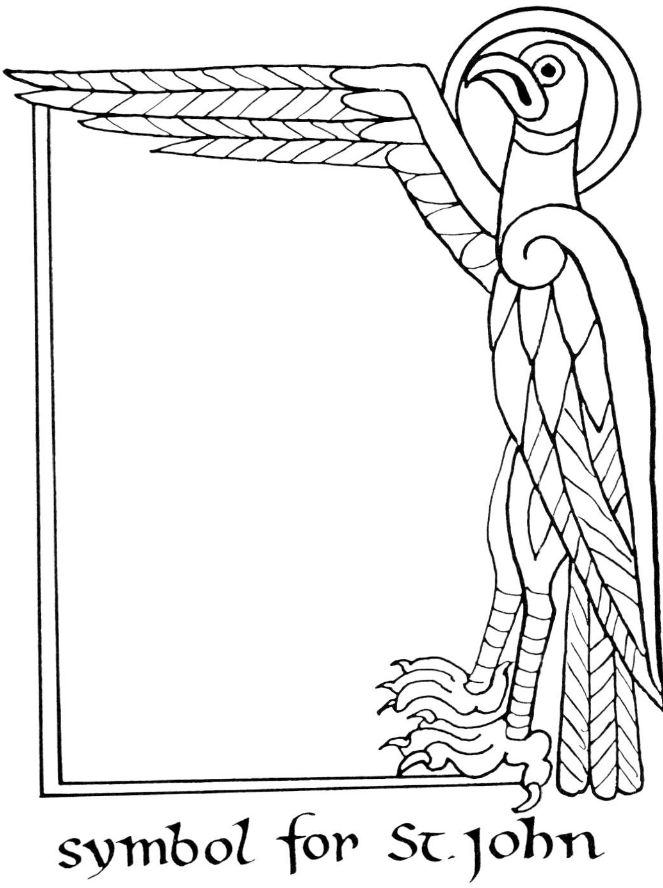

symbol for St. John

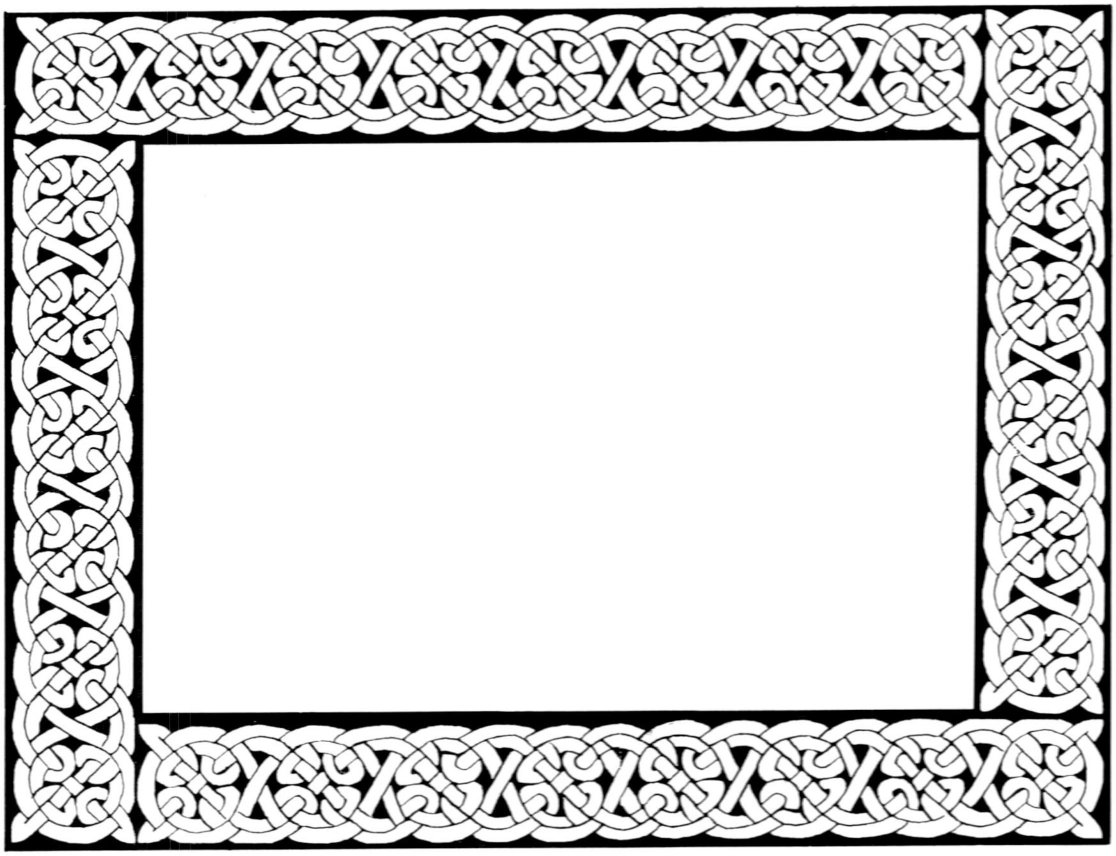

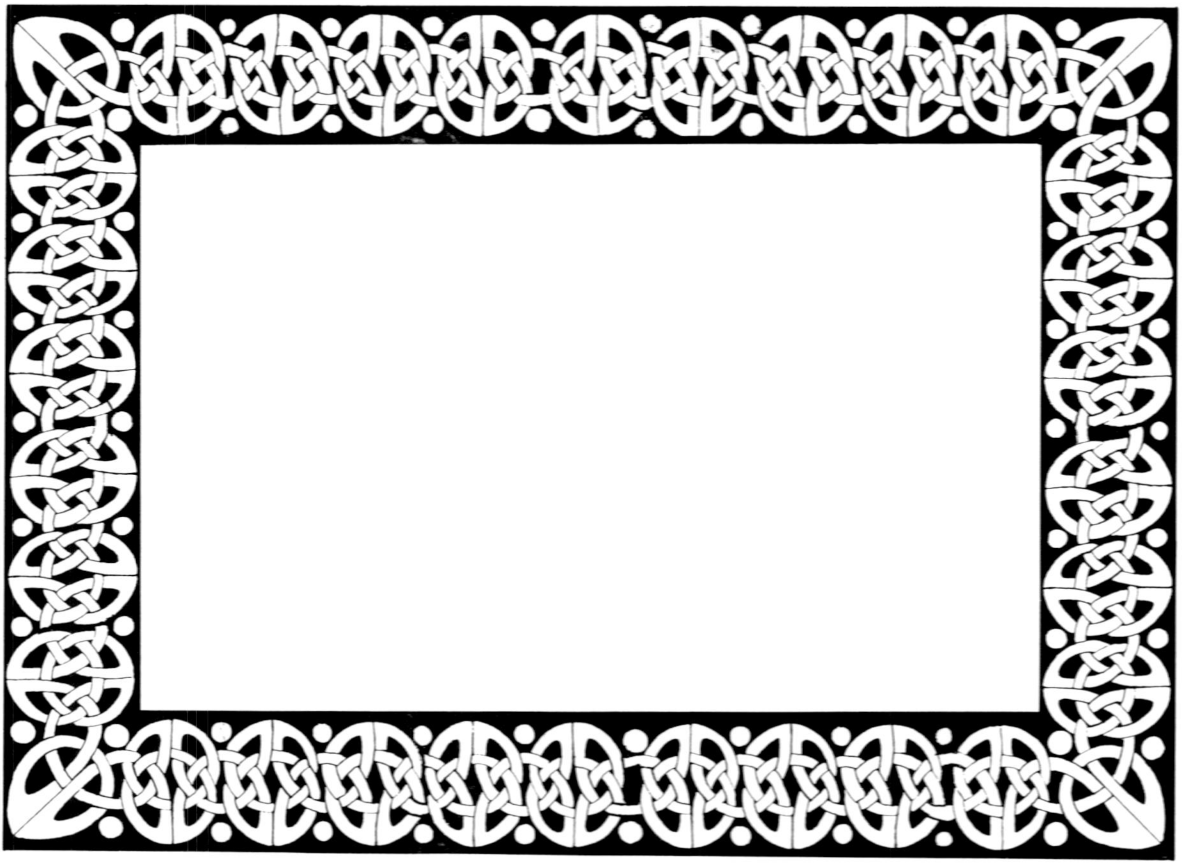

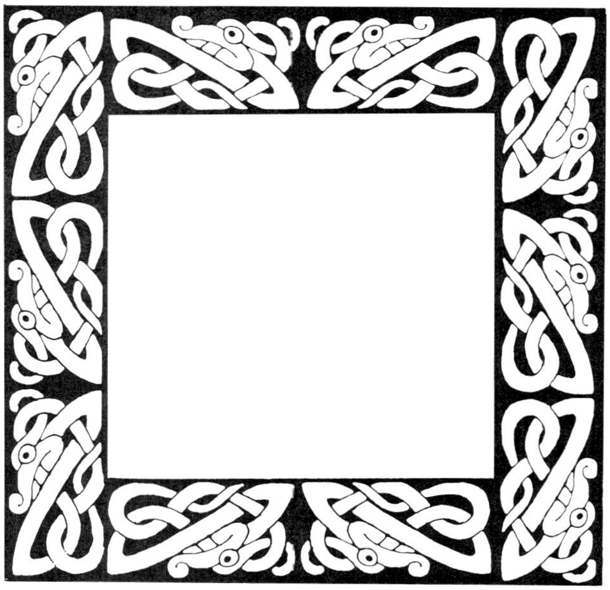

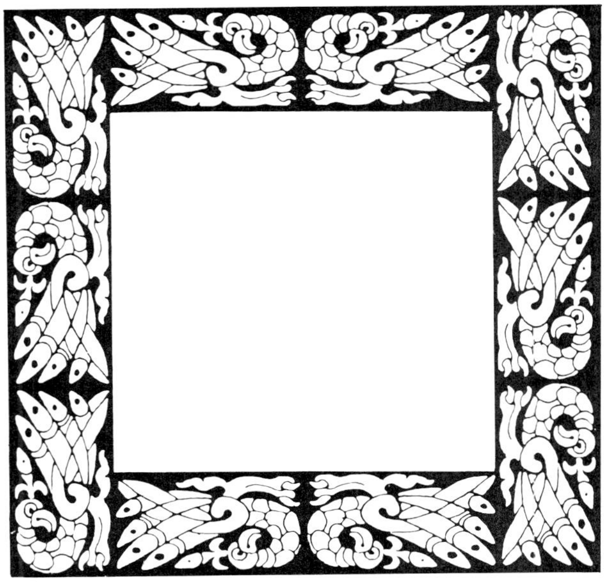

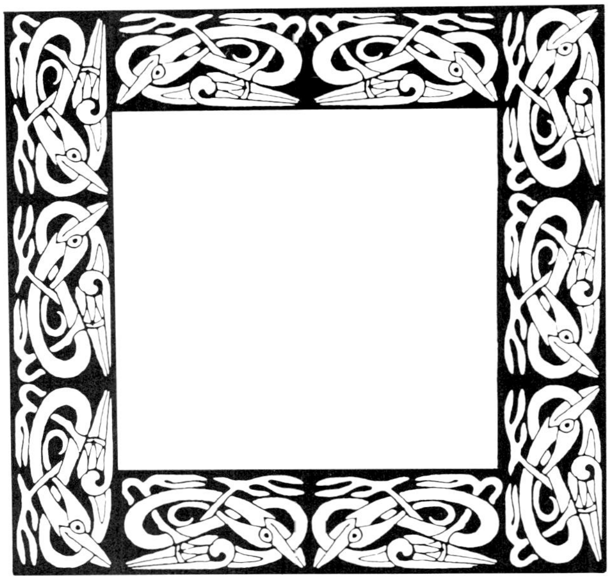

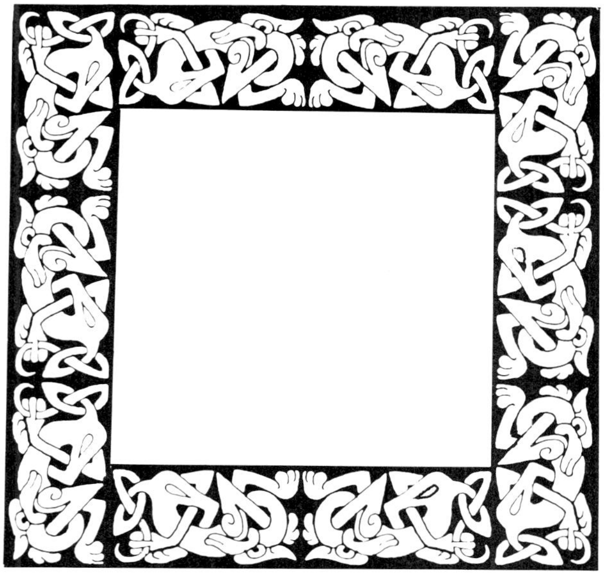

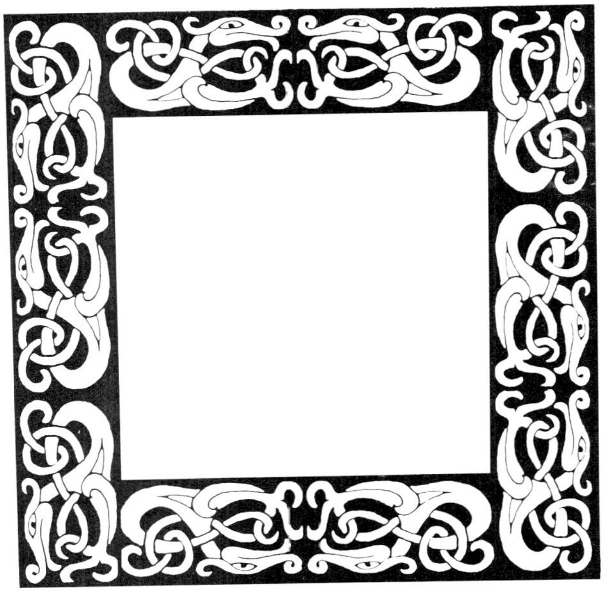

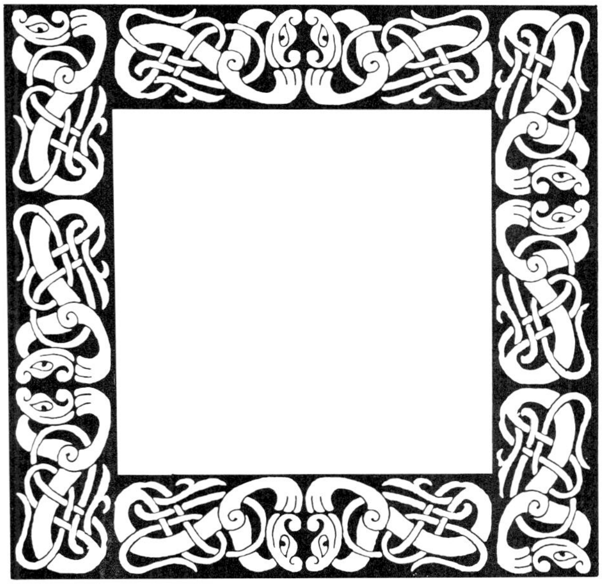

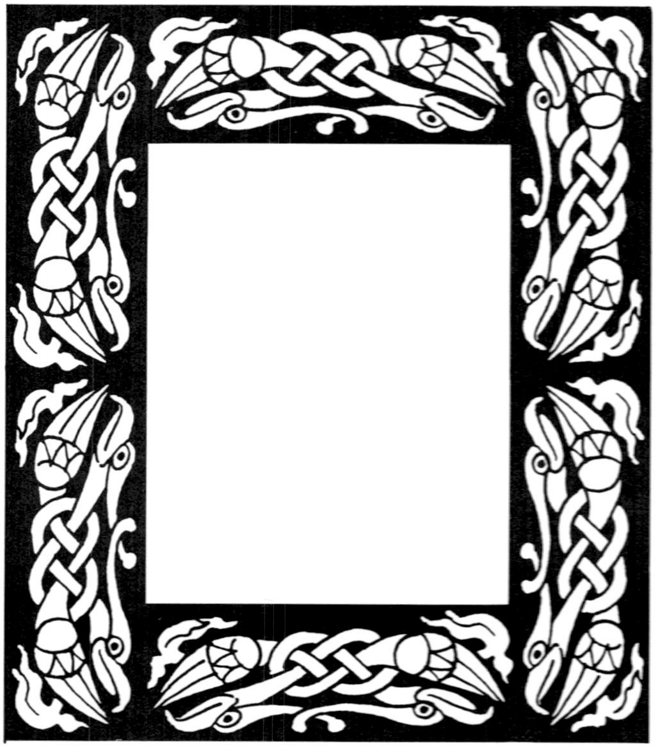

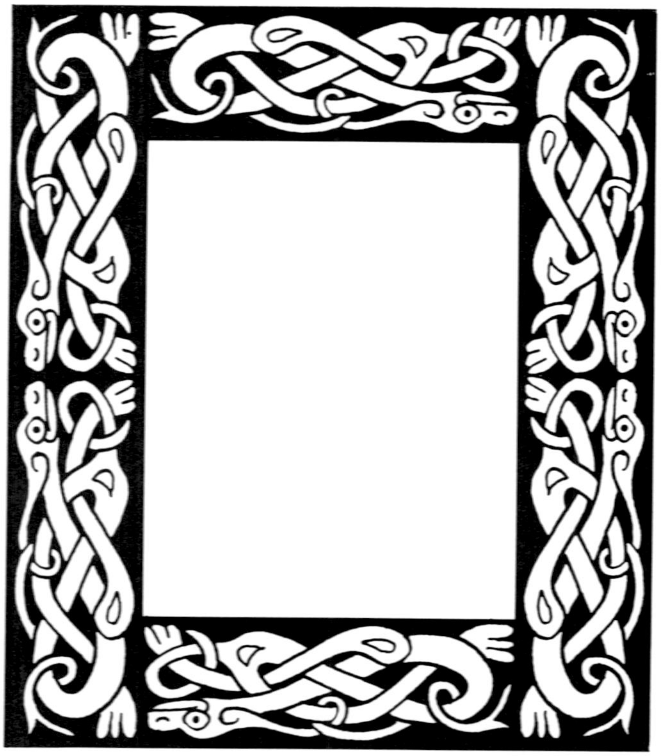

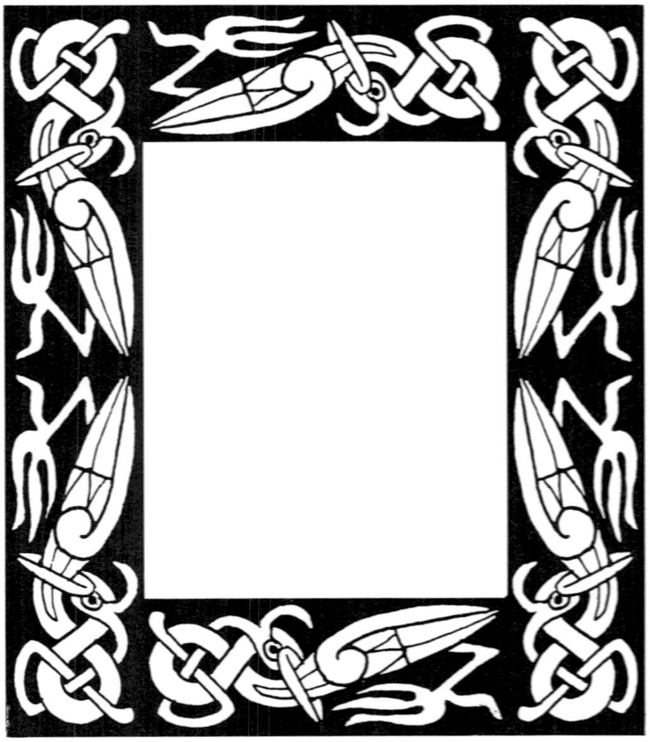

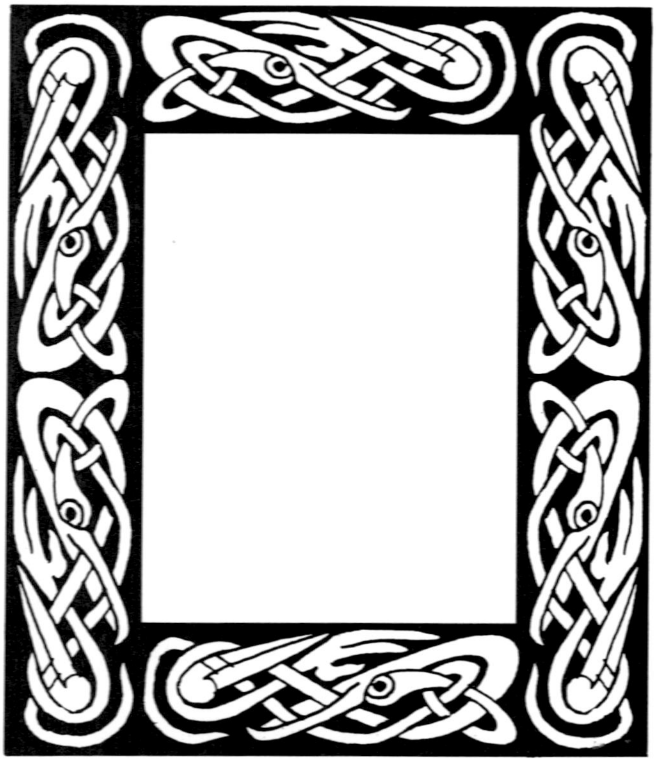

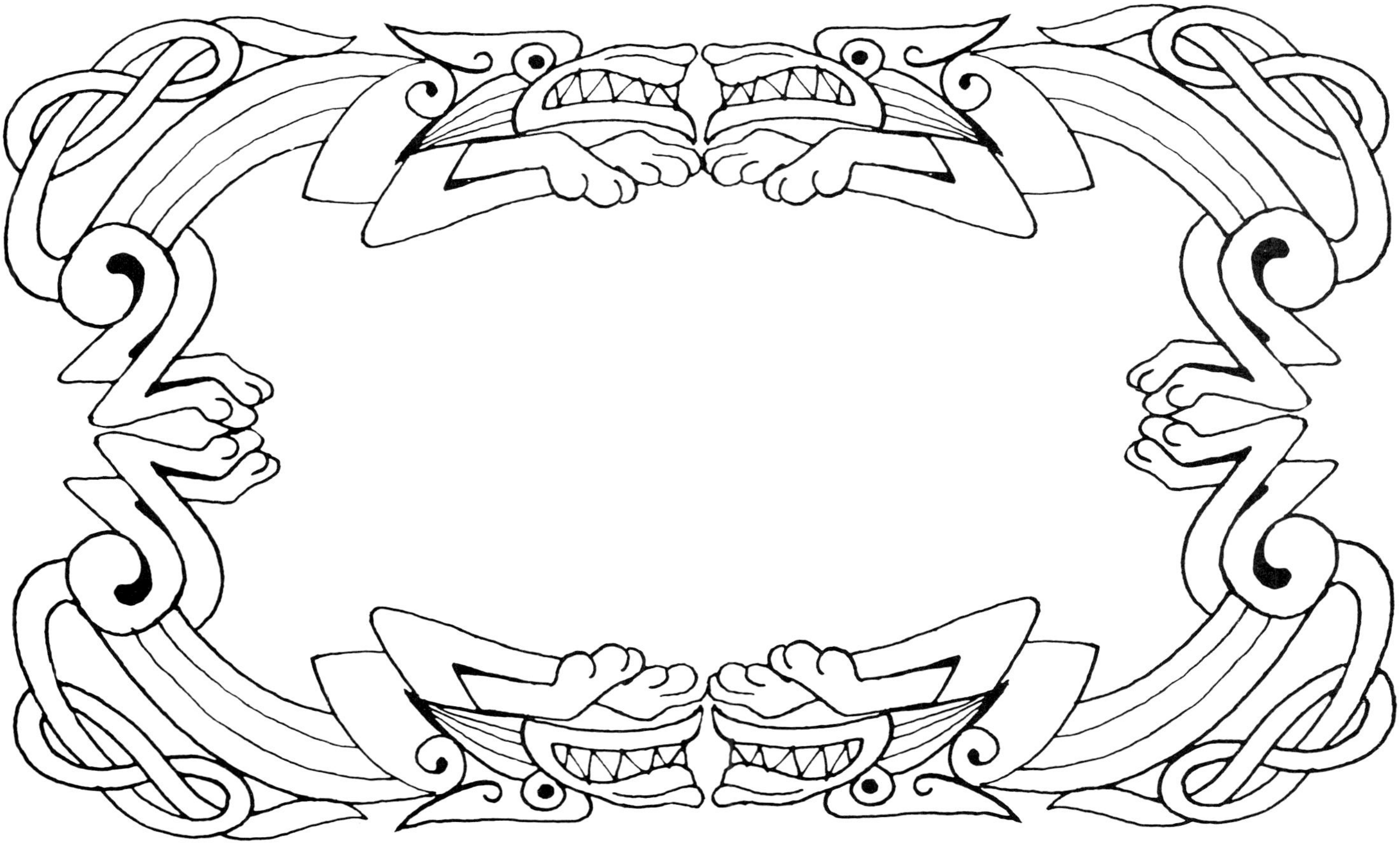

Mallory Pearce